7 HABITS OF
UNCOMMON
Achievers

KATE McVEIGH

First Printing 2005
ISBN 0-89276-968-8

In the U.S. write:
Kenneth Hagin
Ministries
P.O. Box 50126
Tulsa, OK 74150-0126
1-888-28-FAITH
www.rhema.org

In Canada write:
Kenneth Hagin Ministries
P.O. Box 335, Station D
Etobicoke (Toronto),
Ontario
Canada, M9A 4X3

CONTENTS

INTRODUCTION

I am so glad you are reading this book! I don't believe it is by accident that you came across it. Why? Because God has a great plan for your life!

Wherever you are in life right now, your habits brought you to this place, whether good or bad. And with God's help and love, your life can change for the better starting now . . . by changing your habits. You do that one day at a time, little by little.

Did you know that what you do daily determines what you become permanently? Your daily habits are creating your future. You are a result today of yesterday's habits, good or bad. This is true in every area of

> Your daily habits are creating your future.

life. For example, your physical health and the condition and shape of your body are the direct result of yesterday's eating habits—and last year's, and the last 10 years'! The *you* that you have created is a result of your eating habits, exercise habits, and nutrition habits (or lack thereof!)

The same thing is true concerning your finances. Whatever financial situation you may find yourself in at this present moment is a direct result of your past financial habits. Your giving, saving, and spending habits have created your present financial state.

The same is true spiritually speaking. The spiritual condition you are in now is a direct result of your habits. Your Bible reading, church attendance, and prayer habits have created the spiritual condition you are in right now.

But the good news is, you can change your habits! The good habits you begin to form today can change your life for the better in every one of these areas. You decide your daily habits, and your daily habits determine what your future will be. The secret to your future success is hidden in your day-to-day routine. In other words, what you do day in and day out determines what you become.

We are all creatures of habit. Do most of your days follow a typical order of events? Do you ever find yourself in the middle of some type of mindless habitual behavior? Do you have some unhealthy lifestyle habits that you need to change?

> The secret to your future success is hidden in your day-to-day routine.

We often think negatively when we hear the word *habit*, but some habits can be good. There are good habits as well as bad habits. As you study the lives of successful people, you will see a thread of consistency that weaves through their lives—*good* habits they practiced that caused them to succeed. People who have a habit of being diligent, whether at work, at home, or in their own business, end up prospering in what they do.

PROVERBS 10:4

4 He becometh poor that dealeth with a slack hand: but the hand of the diligent maketh rich.

PROVERBS 12:24

24 The hand of the diligent shall bear rule: but the slothful shall be under tribute.

PROVERBS 22:29

29 Seest thou a man diligent in his business? he shall stand before kings; he shall not stand before mean [ordinary] men.

What exactly are habits and how are they developed? Human behavior experts say that it takes 21 days to form a habit. Almost any behavior can usually be changed in just 21 days! *Merriam-Webster's Collegiate Dictionary, 11th Edition,* defines the word *habit* as "a behavior pattern acquired by frequent repetition or physiologic exposure that shows itself in regularity or increased facility of performance; an acquired mode of behavior that has become nearly or completely involuntary; a way of acting fixed through repetition." In other words, a habit is doing the same thing consistently so that eventually you do it without thinking.

For example, you brush your teeth every day, don't you? You probably don't even think about it. It's not a big deal. Through the years, you formed this habit and now it just comes naturally.

Years ago I developed the habit of exercising at least 30 minutes a day and sometimes more, depending on my schedule. But no matter what, I do it at least four times a week, because I like the way it makes me feel. Really, for me it's not hard. I actually enjoy it. I developed this habit at a very young age because I was involved in sports, and I just continued the habit as I grew up.

There are other habits I've developed that I don't always enjoy as much. But I like the results they produce.

Our habits really do influence us more powerfully than we know. Even the habit of being disciplined and planning your day can make an extraordinary impact on your level of success.

For the sake of illustration, let's compare two imaginary women. Mary is a planner. She gets up early every single day to spend time in the Word of God. She makes a point of praying about her job and relationships, and she is always on time for work. She also sets aside additional time to be in God's presence, praising and worshiping Him every day, and is actively involved in her church.

Pat jumps out of bed each morning—only after her alarm clock has already gone off three times—hurries to shower, dresses as quickly as possible, grabs the car keys, and speeds away to work. She is totally frazzled and praying that all the traffic lights will be green. She arrives at the office completely stressed out and totally unprepared for the day ahead.

Pat's productivity is limited because her life is cluttered and rushed and her mind is racing. Because she didn't plan ahead, she has lost her peace. She's entangled with hurry, worry, deadlines, and other pressures.

To make her life easier and more productive, Pat could develop a habit of spending some time with God before leaving the house. Just leaving 10 minutes earlier to allow for an unexpected phone call or a traffic jam would make things so much easier and relieve her of unnecessary stress.

Although these women share some common characteristics—family background, education, profession, and relationships with others—they are two distinctly different people with very different levels of success. The habits that Mary and Pat each practice determine the level of their ultimate success in life.

I've observed some very successful men and women in both the natural and spiritual realms. There are certain things I've watched them do in order to reach the levels of success they now enjoy. Success didn't just fall on them automatically. They had a part to play.

Many times that part has involved years of just doing the same things over and over: reading, meditating, studying, praying, showing up, giving, developing a lifestyle of self-control and discipline, exercising leadership skills, and reaching out to others. The list varies, depending on their particular calling in life.

Some people stand back and look with envy at the success of their peers and say things like, "I'd love to have a successful business like theirs." Or they wonder, "Why is that church (or ministry) so successful?" There usually are reasons. Often we want the success of others, but we don't want to pay the price they paid to get there. We know that success for the

Christian involves following God's plan for our lives and totally obeying His Word (Isa. 1:19).

The principle that godly habits produce welcome results has been called many things. "Seedtime and harvest," "reaping what you sow," and "what goes around, comes around" are just a few of the phrases people often use.

The bottom line is this: discipline yourself to do the right thing long enough, and eventually the right thing will happen to you. Often people get tired of doing the right thing and they give up. The Bible says that you will reap if you faint not (Gal. 6:9).

Are you ready for something good to take place in your life? Are you tired of not living your life to the fullest? Do you want to move beyond the ordinary? Do you want to get out of the rut you've been stuck in? Do you want to live an uncommon life, making an extraordinary impact on the lives of others? Well, you can! You can be all that God has called you to be, and you can reach your full potential.

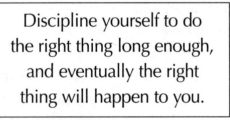

Discipline yourself to do the right thing long enough, and eventually the right thing will happen to you.

Through the years I have noticed how these seven simple, yet powerful, habits have changed people's lives forever. Those who have developed these habits have become successful, and so can you!

I am praying that this book will stir you to realize and grasp the exuberant, abundant life that you were meant to live! You may want to enlist some friends to read this book with you. I encourage you to make this book your own—

write in it, underline, highlight, use the progress chart at the back. Make it personal.

I have made space for you at the end of each chapter so you can take action and write your own journal of success— things from each chapter that speak to you and things you want to remember to put into action in your life. I've also included a 21-day progress chart at the end of the book to help you form new habits. Let's believe together according to Matthew 18:19 for the formation of successful habits in your life. As we believe and doubt not, nothing will be impossible!

As you begin to establish these seven habits, and others God may give you, you can become an uncommon achiever. I am sure you've heard the saying, "If you want something you've never had, you must do what you've never done."

In the following chapters, we are going to discuss and learn how to develop these powerful, life-changing habits of uncommon achievers. As you incorporate these habits into your everyday life, I believe you will never be the same.

Are you ready? Let's go!

Take Action Now

Lord, please help me change the following habits as I read this book:

_____

_____

_____

_____

_____

_____

_____

Lord, please help me develop the following new habits as I read this book:

(Examples: _Read the Bible every day. Pray 15 minutes a day. Speak God's Word over my family every day. Exercise four times a week._)

_____

_____

_____

_____

_____

_____

_____

Write the Vision

Write the vision, and make it plain upon tables,
that he may run that readeth it.
—Habakkuk 2:2

I get so excited about this subject of writing down our visions, dreams, and goals. The reason is, I know that by writing things down, it really works! I have heard some people say that it works like magic. Why do they say that? Because you can't argue with results. No, it's definitely not magic. It's the Bible! When you put spiritual principles into operation, they work for you, no matter who you are.

My life changed drastically several years ago as I listened to a sermon by a pastor friend who shared the importance of writing down your vision and what would happen as a result. He shared all the great things that happened in his own life and ministry as a result of putting his dreams and goals on paper.

His message so motivated and stirred me that I began to act on it immediately. I wrote down my dreams and goals, studied goal setting and planning, and read about others who regularly wrote things down. The results I discovered were amazing.

One study I heard about said the chances of things happening for people who write things down are much greater than for those who don't. This study had absolutely nothing to do with churchgoers or the Bible. It just looked at the average person. These people didn't pray or use any Scripture. Things just happened for them because they wrote them down! I believe the reason this works is because it is a biblical principle.

Another study I read was about a group of college graduates. It was discovered at their 10-year reunion that about two percent of the graduates had more money than all the rest of the class combined. The common denominator among that two percent was *goal setting*. In other words, the top two percent had written down their goals during college and continued to write them down. They were the *only* ones who wrote down goals, and it was determined that this is what caused them to be more successful than the other graduates.

One multimillionaire I read about attributed her success to writing down on a yellow legal pad six things she wanted to accomplish each day. What stood out to me was the fact that she wrote down just six things each day, not 100 things. Being able to scratch six things off your list each day will give you a feeling of accomplishment. Then you can move on to the rest of the things you need to do.

What holds a special place in your heart? Write it down on paper. What do you want to do for God? What unlocks your compassion? Write it down. Your goals can also be what you'd like to own, places you'd like to visit, things you would like to have, people you would like to meet, and so forth.

One way to know what you are called to do in life is to ask yourself what excites you. Does the thought of writing a book excite you? Or maybe having a huge family excites you. It may be starting your own business, owning property, traveling the world, playing a sport, preaching the Gospel, or something else. What is it that gets you going? That is probably a clue pointing to something you are called to do.

Have a Plan and Work the Plan

You must have a detailed plan of action and then focus on working your plan. That is what setting goals is all about. Of course, ask God to lead you to write down His plan for your life. The idea here is to get you moving. These goals can be altered, tweaked, and interrupted by God at any time, but having a plan helps you remain focused.

Let's take a look at the following scriptures:

PROVERBS 16:9 (*TLB*)
9 We should make plans—counting on God to direct us.

ECCLESIASTES 5:3 (*Amplified*)
3 For a dream comes with much business and painful effort.

Setting Goals

What actually is a goal? One definition is, "an ongoing pursuit of a desired outcome until it is accomplished." You may have heard of something called "S.M.A.R.T. goals."[i] These goal characteristics are something to keep in mind when writing goals. Here are some ideas of S.M.A.R.T. goals:

S = Specific. Be specific about what you want. For example, one of your goals may be to put your child through college. Or it may be to become more physically fit and healthy by losing weight.

M = Measurable. Establish weekly or monthly steps you can follow toward reaching your goal. For example, "I will invest $100 a month toward the final amount it will take to put my child through college 10 years from now."

AR = Attainable and **Realistic.** This means that your goals are out of reach (at the moment) but not out of sight. Set goals for yourself that are a challenge, but on the other hand, you don't want to set goals that are completely unreasonable. For example, it's discouraging to say, "I will lose 25 pounds in one week." You must be realistic about it.

T = Time-defined. If you are able, create a deadline for your plan of action (not counting miracles). In other words, you may want to set 10-year goals, five-year goals, one-year goals, six-month goals, and one-month goals. One great man of God said that it's better to set a whole lot of goals and reach only half of them than to have no goals and reach all of them.

Little Actions Produce
Significant Savings

The following is an example of how a "little" action can save you thousands of dollars by paying off a house early. Financial planners tell us that if you were to make just one extra house payment a year on an average 30-year loan (depending on your interest rate and other factors), you would cut roughly seven years of payments off your loan! In other words, you would pay your house off in 23 years instead of 30.

Let's say your house payment was $1,500 a month. If you made one extra payment a year, you would pay an extra $34,500 over 23 years. But by paying off your home seven years early, you would *save* $126,000 in payments!

There are also biweekly payment plans available. You pay half of your monthly payment every two weeks, which adds up to 26 half-payments in a year. That equals 13 full payments. This way, you're able to make the extra payment a little at a time throughout the year instead of all at once.

If these strategies work, then why don't more people use them? They either don't know about them or they just haven't disciplined themselves to get in the habit of putting them into practice. These approaches are a small price to pay for big results. (Check with your own mortgage company to find out exact details regarding your situation, as each case is different.)

Now don't forget "the God factor." He could move in a big way and enable you to pay your home off in even less time. But these are just some practical suggestions, some things you can do now to bring about a significant savings.

Write 'SMART' Goals

When writing your goals, ask yourself, "Are these 'SMART' goals? Are they Specific, Measurable, Attainable, Realistic, and Time-defined?" The following is an example of creating SMART goals for finances. This is just a very general example of what someone's SMART goals may be:

• I will tithe (give 10 percent of my income) to my church and honor God in my finances.

• I will be out of credit card debt in one year, or as soon as I can be. I will do this by paying an extra $100 each month. I will call my credit card company and ask them to lower my interest rate. I will cut up the rest of my credit cards and pay cash until I am out of debt. I will not buy things I cannot pay for.

• I will meet with a financial planner twice a year to formulate a plan for my financial future. I will establish a will or a living trust for my family.

• I will read three books on investing this year. I will read Kate McVeigh's book *Conquering Intimidation* (smile). I will pray for God to lead me to a financial mentor so I can learn to use more wisdom with my money.

• I will save a certain amount (after giving to God) out of every paycheck.

Three Practical Habits
for Financial Blessing

My mother was a woman of great wisdom and she instilled—or should I say drilled—into me some practical money habits when I was just a teenager going to Bible school.

At the time, I was broke; I didn't have a dime. Let me tell you, it wasn't always easy. But I am blessed today because of these habits. The greatest money habit my mother developed in me was the habit of waiting until I had the money to pay for things, rather than getting into credit card debt like most Americans do today.

Thanks be to God, I have never paid interest on a credit card in my life! I have never been in credit card debt, ever! It wasn't always fun waiting, and building a savings account didn't happen overnight. I still practice these habits today and am blessed as a result.

You may not have incorporated any of these habits into your life yet. You may be in debt, but don't let that keep you down. Work toward establishing the following three key habits to help you gain financial victory:

1. Make it a habit . . . to always give God your tithe (10 percent) out of each paycheck you receive, and then sow offerings above that as He directs (Mal. 3:10–11).

2. Make it a habit . . . to save a certain amount of money every month (no matter how small). Consider it as important as a bill.

3. Make it a habit . . . to no longer pay interest to your credit card company. If you can't pay it off in full at the end of the month, don't buy it.

Write Down Your Goals

At the beginning of every year, I write down all the things I am believing God for. I list places I want to go, vacations I want to take, things I might want to own, and even people I'd like to meet. (Did you know that there is scientific evidence that we may all be about six people away from meeting anyone in the world?)

There may be someone you want to meet. Write their name down on your list. You may want to write down an amount of money you desire to sow into the Kingdom of God. Perhaps you desire a closer walk with the Lord, your spouse, or your children. One of my goals is to become more excellent in all I do for God. I desire to be a better leader and to develop a stronger love walk. I also have on my list to lead over one million souls to Christ. It costs nothing to dream on paper, so write down those things that are in your heart.

One year, after listening to the sermon I mentioned earlier, I was so motivated that I grabbed a piece of paper and immediately wrote down 67 things.

When writing my goals, I also sensed the Lord challenging me to write down anything in my life that would require a miracle. These things would be a little different from goals. For example, you may set a goal to lose five pounds, and you can do that on your own, with God's help. Losing five pounds wouldn't require a miracle. Goals like that are good, and you should write them down.

However, you should also write down the things you want God to do in your life that you *can't* do for yourself, like healing your body, sending you a spouse, or giving you supernatural favor.

That particular year, after writing down my 67 things, I then wrote down fourteen simply incredible things that would require a miracle, including places where I wanted to preach, a family member who needed deliverance, and a television station I wanted to be on. After I wrote those things down, the most amazing thing happened. Thirteen out of the fourteen "simply incredible" things I listed, as well as 40 of the 67 things on my other list, came to pass in the first three months of that year! It was totally awesome seeing these things come to pass like they did. I didn't do anything different, other than . . . *I wrote it down.*

These days, we hear a lot about goal setting and finding creative ways to achieve those goals. Proverbs 14:8 says, *"The wisdom of the prudent is to understand his way: but the folly of fools is deceit."* Uncommon achievers—like Jesus—know their purpose in life. Jesus said great things, and many of the things He said are recorded in the Gospels. Someone wrote them down.

The Bible reveals to us that God is a planner! The Book of Jeremiah says, " 'For I know the plans I have for you,' declares the Lord, 'plans to prosper you and not to harm you, plans to give you hope and a future' " (Jer. 29:11 *NIV*). God has a great plan and purpose for your life!

Write Your Own Mission Statement

Have you defined your purpose in life? Do you have a mission statement for yourself? If not, you can start by sitting down and making a list of those things about which you are passionate.

It isn't difficult at all to see the purpose of some people's lives. They are so focused on their purpose that every time you see them, they talk about it. For some people, their purpose is world missions. For others, it's youth ministry. Some people are called to work with children or start their own business. Still others are highly motivated to be a good spouse and raise a wonderful family.

Your own mission statement expresses what you want to be and what you want to do with your life. It can quickly become the added basis for helping measure everything in your life.

A while back I enlisted a professional who helped me write my mission statement. He helped me put in writing what was in my heart. You don't have to be the head of a ministry or corporation or the pastor of a church to have a mission statement. You just need to think about what God has put in your heart and write it down. It doesn't have to be very long—maybe just a paragraph or two.

Here is an example of a little saying I have on my ministry letters and other publications: "Kate McVeigh Ministries . . . touching the world with God's power and love." This saying, as well as my mission statement, reveals my mission in life. It's what I feel God has called me to do. God has called you to do something great for Him. Now go for it. Put down on paper what's in your heart. Don't be discouraged if it takes a few weeks or even months to get your mission statement to a place where you feel comfortable with it—where it *defines* you.

Uncommon Achievers Continue to Set Goals

Keep in mind that setting goals is not just a one-time exercise. Once you achieve goals, you set other goals and adjust them from time to time as needed. Goal setting is an ongoing project.

What excites you? Write it down! What stimulates you into action? Write it down! What is really important to you? Write it down! God has a good plan for your life. You may be surprised at what you write on that piece of paper. Look it over carefully. Make the necessary adjustments after you pray over your list.

Grow comfortable with yourself. Don't be afraid to add new and better goals to your list. Allow yourself to dream big, and don't think that anything is too far out or beyond your ability to accomplish. Nothing is impossible with God! Remember, He has a purpose for your life. He can bring to pass every dream in your heart!

I said earlier that I once wrote down 67 things I wanted to accomplish. I went back over that long list recently, and about 65 of those 67 things I had written down have already come to pass in my life. As a matter of fact, while I was completing this book, something I had on my list came to pass. I always wanted to own a baby grand piano so I could worship the Lord at home. Not long ago, someone felt led to bless me with a beautiful baby grand piano.

Don't let money stop you from dreaming. It costs you nothing to write down your dream. I'm sure there are some things you wouldn't mind owning if you didn't have to pay for them. Put them down on paper. Something happens when you write them down.

I heard a story recently about the late comedian George Burns. In his mid-90s he was planning and writing down what he wanted at his 100th birthday party. He said that what you plan for and schedule usually shows up. And he made it to his 100th birthday party.

I encourage you right now to write down in the "Take Action Now" section at the end of this chapter, five miracles that you would like to see take place in your life this year. Maybe you want your kids to come back to the Lord. Perhaps you want to go back to college. Make a note of something you'd like to do. List places where you'd like to vacation. Include a home or vehicle you might like to own and a job promotion you'd like to have, or perhaps a business you'd like to start. Maybe even include how many souls you want to win to the Lord this year.

Just start writing down things as they pop into your mind. As I said earlier, when writing down your goals, write down anything you want to own, do, dream, become, or have. Just begin dreaming on paper. Have fun! Here are some examples:

1. Move to a nicer neighborhood with good schools for my children

2. Vacation in Hawaii

3. Give more to missions than I ever have before

4. Meet Kate McVeigh (smile)

5. Lose weight and have a brand-new wardrobe

6. Own a vacation home

7. Win five people to the Lord this year

8. *(Keep going . . . . Don't be afraid to dream big!)*

Do you realize what the Bible really is? It's God's own written-down plan and vision for the entire universe. If God wrote down His vision, shouldn't you?

You will be absolutely, utterly amazed at what will happen as a result of writing down your vision. Some of the most uncommon achievers in the world are people who write down their goals, dreams, and vision. So begin the habit today of writing things down and watch your dreams become realities. You have those dreams inside you; now put them down on paper! You've learned a secret . . . just watch what God can do.

Take Action Now

My dreams, goals, and miracles:

_____

_____

_____

_____

_____

_____

_____

_____

_____

_____

_____

_____

_____

_____

_____

_____

[1] S.M.A.R.T. goals are attributed to Paul J. Meyer of Paul J. Meyer Resources, Waco, Texas. This list is adapted from his.

Develop a Prayer Habit

What things soever ye desire, when ye pray,
believe that ye receive them, and ye shall have them.
—Mark 11:24

During my travels over the past several years, I have discovered one universal truth: Great men and women of God have a habit of spending time with their Heavenly Father. They have a prayer habit!

PSALM 119:164
164 Seven times a day do I praise thee because of thy righteous judgments.

DANIEL 6:10
10 He [Daniel] kneeled upon his knees three times a day, and prayed, and gave thanks before his God.

In Psalm 119:164, David declared that it was his practice to pray seven times a day. Daniel had a habit of praying three times a day. And throughout his letters, the Apostle Paul reveals that he, too, had a great prayer life.

We also know that Jesus had a habit of praying. The Bible says He left the disciples and crowds of people and *"went up into a mountain apart to pray"* (Matt. 14:23). The Gospel writers show that He did that often. It is vitally important that you and I "come apart to pray" before we come apart altogether! It's been said, "Seven days without prayer makes one weak."

What caused these men to be so successful? They had a prayer habit! Prayer was the power source behind their success. Prayer is the key to *your* suc-

> "Seven days without prayer makes one weak."

cess as well. Never underestimate the power of prayer.

Daily prayer is an important habit that we should develop in our lives. We must have regular, genuine communication with God. It's important to set aside a specific time to pray each day. It doesn't necessarily have to be the same time every day, as long as you pray! I have found, however, that praying for your day first thing in the morning helps the day run much smoother.

Every morning and night, I plead the blood of Jesus over my family and my ministry. Each morning, I ask God for favor and for wisdom in everything I do, and I thank Him for His divine protection. This has become a habit.

Maybe you have a half-hour commute to work in the morning. Why not take advantage of that time and pray? It could be your time alone with God. You don't necessarily have to be kneeling in a room to pray, although you can be. If you have children running around the house, for example, that might be a little hard for you. The whole idea is just to pray at some point every day. Just do it!

Mastering Distractions

Often when we purpose in our heart to set aside time to spend with God, the devil tries to interrupt us with distractions. He does this because he knows how powerful prayer can be. Have you ever purposed in your heart to spend time with the Lord, and even though your phone hasn't rung all day, right when you start to pray, it rings? Or, when you finally begin to pray, do you suddenly think of a ton of important things you forgot to do?

Here's what I've learned to do. I take a pad of paper with me when I pray. It helps to free up my mind from distractions. When I suddenly think of something important to do, instead of thinking about it during my whole prayer time and being distracted, I simply write it down. Then my mind is freed up to pray without interruption.

Another good reason to bring a notebook or paper with you during your prayer time is so you can be prepared to write down anything the Lord may say to you.

God wants to speak to you and give you supernatural ideas and guidance. John 10:27 says, *"My sheep hear my voice . . . ,"* and John 16:13 says, *". . . he will shew you things to come."* Make this your confession: "I hear the voice of the Good Shepherd, and He leads and guides me."

Expect Answers When You Pray

When we pray, we're not just speaking words and blowing hot air. We are praying to our Heavenly Father with purpose, expecting to get answers.

When I was growing up in Michigan, my sister and I went to a store called "Hit or Miss." Its name was an apt description of that store because you could go there at any given time and find something inexpensive, but when you got it home and put it on, suddenly you found that it had a hole under the arm. Guess what? You "missed."

On the other hand, sometimes you could find very high-quality items at relatively low prices, and there was absolutely nothing wrong with them. That meant you "hit."

I sometimes think that people approach prayer that way. It's "hit or miss." They feel that sometimes their prayers will be answered and other times they won't be. They think, *Maybe I'll "hit" it this time.*

Prayer is not supposed to be a gamble, where you may or may not win. That is not the way God wants you to approach prayer. He wants your prayers to "hit" every time. The purpose of prayer is to believe that your prayers will be answered every time you pray. If you keep that in mind—that your prayers will be answered—prayer becomes exciting!

> The purpose of prayer is to believe that your prayers will be answered every time you pray.

How do we know that our prayers will be answered? Because the following scripture says so!

1 JOHN 5:14–15
14 And this is the confidence that we have in him, that, if we ask any thing according to his will, he heareth us:

15 And if we know that he hear us, whatsoever we ask, we know that we have the petitions that we desired of him.

This scripture reveals to us that if we ask anything according to God's will, He hears us, and that we will receive whatever we ask Him for. The key here is to ask according to God's will.

How do we know the will of God for our lives? Well, the answer to that is simple. The will of God is the Word of God. So we could read that scripture like this: ". . . if we ask anything according to His Word, He hears us."

When Jesus prayed or spoke healing over someone's body, He never one time said, "Father, if it's Your will, heal them." That's because Jesus knew it was God's will for all to be healed.

There is one account in the New Testament during which Jesus did pray, "If it be Thy will." However, Jesus' request did not concern healing or needs being met. It concerned the Father's plan for His life (see Matt. 26:39,42). Jesus prayed this prayer about a life decision.

You may be making a job decision or deciding whether to move to a new city. You can't find "thou shalt move to such-and-such city" in the Bible. So you can tell the Lord that you want His plan and purpose for your life. (If you need to make an important decision right now, read Proverbs 3:5–6 and James 1:5–8).

God's Word Is His Will

Remember, to receive an answer in prayer, we must pray in line with God's will, which is His Word. So it is vitally important that you have scriptures to stand on when you pray. We must pray the Word.

> To receive an answer in prayer, we must pray in line with God's will, which is His Word.

For example, if you need physical healing, you can approach God's throne boldly and stand on First Peter 2:24 which tells us, "By His stripes, you were healed."

And you might also stand on Matthew 8:17 which says, "Himself took our infirmities, and bore our sicknesses." There are many more healing scriptures you can stand on, including Isaiah 53:4–5, Psalm 103:3, and Psalm 107:20, just to name a few. [The author has written a minibook on healing entitled *The Doctrine of Healing*, available for $1 through her ministry Web site, **www.katemcveigh.org.**—Ed.]

How Long Should I Pray?

I am often asked, "Kate, how much time do you spend in prayer each day?" The answer varies. There are times when I pray for hours at the Lord's direction. During other seasons in my life, I feel God leading me to spend more time studying the Word than praying. Then there are seasons during which I may spend hours devouring teaching tapes from faith-filled ministers.

We need to be led by the Spirit of God when it comes to how much time we spend in prayer. Don't fall into the trap of comparing your prayer life with someone else's. The Bible says it's not wise to compare ourselves to others (2 Cor. 10:12).

Have you ever been around "Sister Spiritual" who tells you of the hours and hours she spends praying every day

> We need to be led by the Spirit of God when it comes to how much time we spend in prayer.

and then asks you how much time you spend? Let me just say this: First, real people of prayer don't go around bragging about how much time they have spent with God. Second, the Scriptures say that if you're praying to be seen of men, that's the only reward you'll receive (Matt. 6:5).

When I was in Bible school, I briefly lived with a "Sister Spiritual." She would announce to me that she was going to her bedroom to pray for hours, and that she was fasting. She frowned upon me because I liked to watch *Little House on the Prairie* and she tried to make me feel bad for watching it. The thing was, I did pray every day. I just didn't tell her. And that's because we're not supposed to brag about our praying!

What really bugged this girl was that God started opening doors for me to preach and was using me to bless people. This drove her crazy. She couldn't figure out why God was using me in this way. She said she prayed more than I did and thought she was more spiritual than I was. Now I can see that's nothing more than a religious spirit.

Don't ever let the devil make you feel bad because you are not praying like someone else. Just do every day what God is leading you to do. He is not going to ask you to do something that's so hard for you that you can't possibly do it.

How Much Is Enough?

When I was growing up, I had a relative who would always tell me, "Kate, no matter *how many hours you spend* every day in prayer, you could *never* pray enough."

Obviously, this left me feeling like a failure all the time. After I got saved, I kept looking for that statement in the Bible, but I never found that scripture! I found out that that statement was not accurate.

I am aware of the scripture verse that says to pray without ceasing (1 Thess. 5:17). But that is actually referring to an *attitude* of prayer. God knows that you have to take a shower, brush your teeth, and go to work. So it would be impossible for you to literally pray 24 hours a day, 7 days a week, 365 days a year (or as the teenagers say, "24-7-365").

An *attitude of prayer* is having God on your heart and your mind, and talking to Him as much as you can. It's keeping Him in your thoughts and asking Him to help you throughout the day. It's practicing His presence. At work you can ask Him to help you on the job, but you're not necessarily praying out loud about it. He's just with you all day and you're communicating with Him.

I believe we *can* pray enough every day. We can pray the amount the Lord is requiring of each of us. For example, the Lord knows your schedule. He knows if you have children, work, and other responsibilities. You have to be led by the Spirit in your own heart and find out how much prayer God is requiring of you each day. It may even be different from day to day.

The important thing is that you do some praying every day. If you're not in the habit of praying daily, you might want to start with 10 or 15 minutes. Doing this consistently is better than not praying at all.

Often the devil will try to condemn you for not praying longer. Let's say you set aside 20 minutes and prayed. The devil may come along and say, "You should have prayed longer than that. How do you expect to get answers to your prayers when you don't pray any longer than 20 minutes?" He may even try to quote a scripture out of context—for example, Matthew 26:40. He may say, "Can't you even pray one hour?" Don't listen to the devil's lies!

I have found that spending 10 or 15 minutes in concentrated prayer is much more effective than praying a whole hour with my mind thinking about doing the laundry or halfway falling asleep. Shorter prayers that are full of faith can be more effective. It's the *prayer of faith* that changes things, not just the amount of time you pray (see James 5:14–15). Ten minutes of praying in faith is more powerful than 10 hours of praying in unbelief.

> Ten minutes of praying in faith is more powerful than 10 hours of praying in unbelief.

Prayer Is the Key That Unlocks Our Victory

When you begin to see the results that prayer produces, you will probably get even more excited about spending time with God. Prayer really is the key that unlocks our victory.

I remember the time I heard one minister say, "Failure in any Christian endeavor is a prayer failure." What a true statement that is!

Whenever we launch out in a new area to do something big and it doesn't go over well, we need to trace it right back to the prayer room. Did we pray beforehand? Did we spend enough time in prayer? Did we sense a "release" to proceed? Did we have a feeling that we should wait a while? Prayer can clear up all the questions and pave the way to victory.

Discipline Yourself to Pray

It takes discipline to produce good habits, and good habits produce good results. If you look at the background of the word *disciple*, it refers to "a disciplined one."

Discipline is defined in *Merriam-Webster's Collegiate Dictionary* as "training that corrects, molds, or perfects the mental faculties or moral character; . . . orderly or pre-scribed conduct or pattern of behavior; self-control." [i]

Remember, discipline often is doing something you don't like to do in order to create something you love. If you want something you've never had, you have to do something you've never done. For instance, you might not like working out, but you love the results it produces.

We must realize that we need a disciplined prayer habit in order to succeed in life. You may not *feel* like getting up a littler earlier in the morning to pray for 15 or 20 minutes. You may not *feel* like spending time reading your Bible

> Discipline often is doing something you don't like to do in order to create something you love.

every day. But believe me, you will love the results these activities produce. As a matter of fact, they will produce great things in your life, such as:
- Joy (Ps. 16:11)
- Refreshing (Acts 3:19)
- Peace (Isa. 26:3; John 14:27)
- Strength (Neh. 8:10; Isa. 41:10)
- Healing (Prov. 4:20–22)

and much more!

Create a Positive Atmosphere

One thing that I do to help keep myself spiritually fit is to create an atmosphere of faith. One way I do that is by listening to Christian music. Another way is by writing down Bible verses and statements that help build my faith. I've even printed out scriptures and sayings and attached them to my bathroom mirror to keep the Word before my eyes.

When I travel, I may be on an airplane with noise, crying kids, or people talking doubt and unbelief. So what do I do? I create my own atmosphere by putting on headphones and listening to preaching tapes or music to drown out all the negative things around me. I try to take every opportunity I can to put the Word into my heart and mind.

I even have a sermon called "How to Make the Most of Your Layover." I got this when I was stranded in the Chicago airport for eight hours due to a snowstorm. I was tired, and I wanted to go home! I started to get negative and complaining. I called my mother, trying to get her to feel sorry for me being stuck all day in the airport. She said, "Why not make the most of your layover? You could work on new sermons! Write a new book! Catch up on your Bible reading! All sorts of things!"

Her words made an impression on me. Instead of feeling sorry for ourselves, we *can* make the most of our layovers! We can turn a negative situation into a positive one. It's up to us. My pastor used to say, "If life has dealt you a lemon, make lemonade!"

God is also the God of economy. He can get a lot of mileage out of one thing. For example, whenever I exercise, I watch a Christian teaching video. When I'm driving in my car, I pray in the Holy Ghost or listen to tapes. Each day, as I put on my makeup (which takes awhile), I listen to teaching tapes. Just think—if every Christian woman listened to one positive teaching tape each time she put on her makeup or did her hair, in just a short time she would become a powerhouse for God!

Including small amounts of prayer in your daily schedule also adds up quickly. If you make it a habit to pray in the Spirit just 15 minutes each day, at the end of one year's time you will have prayed over 90 hours of God's perfect will for your life!

| Little hinges swing big doors. |

Just imagine what 90 hours of prayer would produce! That 15 minutes of prayer a day might not seem like a long time to you, but little things add up. Little hinges swing big doors.

Realizing the Results Prayer Produces

A lot of people think that laziness is the number one reason why people don't pray. I tend to disagree. I have often found that people who don't pray are not absolutely, positively convinced of the results prayer produces. If they were, they would be praying a whole lot more than they are right now.

Once you begin to see results, it's going to inspire you to pray even more. And the more you do it, the more you will enjoy it.

JAMES 5:16

16 . . . The effectual fervent prayer of a righteous man availeth much.

The Amplified Bible says it this way: ". . . The earnest (heartfelt, continued) prayer of a righteous man makes tremendous power available [dynamic in its working]."

Notice that heartfelt, continued prayer makes available tremendous, dynamic power! If we really understood the tremendous power that is made available to us when we pray, we would have a hard time doing anything else. We would probably be praying a lot more every day!

Ideas for Getting Started

Here are a few ideas to help get you started in prayer.

1. Set the right atmosphere to invite God's presence into your prayer time. Maybe begin by softly playing a worship CD or tape.

2. Kneel, sit in a chair, or even walk around the room. Find a position you're comfortable with. I personally like to walk when I pray.

3. Turn off your phones. You might want to have your Bible open to particular scripture verses you want to pray—for example, the prayers in Ephesians chapters 1 and 3.

Just do what works for you. Please don't misunderstand me: I'm not trying to tell anyone how he or she should pray. I'm just giving you some ideas.

What I am saying is mainly directed toward the person who has never enjoyed a daily prayer life and really wants to know how to get started. These are merely suggestions of ways to develop the habit of setting aside specific time to be alone with the Lord and pray. The Holy Spirit will let you know what to do. Just let Him lead you.

Develop the Habit of Praying in the Spirit

Praying in the Holy Spirit is one of the most powerful, Bible-proven ways you can possibly pray.

ACTS 2:4
4 And they were all filled with the Holy Ghost, and began to speak with other tongues, as the Spirit gave them utterance.

MARK 16:17
17 And these signs shall follow them that believe; . . . they shall speak with new tongues.

Smith Wigglesworth was a great man of God who flowed in tremendous signs and wonders. According to one biography, 14 people were raised from the dead under his ministry. [ii]

When I was 16 years old, I met a preacher who was healed of an incurable brain tumor when Smith Wigglesworth prayed for him. This preacher shared that when people asked Brother Wigglesworth the secret to his success, he answered, "I pray in tongues two hours every day, building *myself* up. Then I go out and build up the people."

What an awesome testimony to the life-changing power of the Holy Spirit! We might want to have the same results Wigglesworth had in his ministry, but we might not be willing to do what he did to get there.

Think about it—if you make a habit of praying in tongues every day, there is no limit to what God can do through you. When you have a habit of praying in the Spirit, you can see great things happen!

Some of the greatest things that have ever happened in my own life and ministry came after I had spent a long period of time praying in other tongues. One time while driving from Colorado to Oklahoma, I was so motivated that I prayed in tongues for 11 straight hours!

I had been listening to some teaching tapes about the benefits of speaking in tongues, and I decided it was high time to act on what I'd heard. I'd just finished preaching and the tape player in my car was broken. I was all by myself, heading back home, and I figured this would be a great opportunity to pray in the Spirit. I purposed in my heart that I would pray in the Holy Spirit all the way home. (I am a goal setter. Setting goals helps motivate me!) I was so excited, thinking I would surely feel some great anointing come upon me.

When I got started, I remember praying for what seemed like a long time. Then I looked at my watch and found I'd only been praying a whopping 20 minutes! I was sure I had been praying for at least three hours! The devil told me this was going to be a long day.

However, I just kept on praying and finally, after 11 hours on the road, I pulled in to my driveway. Immediately a thought popped into my head: *Do you feel edified?*

I answered, "I'm not moved by what I feel because the Bible says, *'He that speaketh in an unknown tongue edifieth himself'* (1 Cor. 14:4). Therefore I believe I'm edified whether I feel like it or not! So, since I'm not moved by what I feel, I am going to take my little edified body to bed right now."

I opened the door to my house, and to my utter amazement, I saw a huge angel standing in my kitchen. I had never seen anything like it! This angel was as tall as my ceiling. (The church I grew up in taught that angels were like little naked babies—chubby, cherub-like beings that floated around with their little wings flapping!)

When I saw this angel, it shocked me. I thought, *Wow, we have big angels encamped round about us for our protection. Praise the Lord!*

During the next several weeks and months after that time of prayer, I experienced some of the greatest miracles I'd ever seen in my ministry to that point. I also had the biggest breakthroughs I'd ever experienced financially, spiritually, and in every other kind of way imaginable. I believe this was a direct result of the 11 hours that I had spent praying in the Holy Ghost.

Get in the habit of praying in the Spirit every day. What's so great about it is that you can be doing other things and building yourself up at the same time. You can pray in the Spirit while cleaning the house, doing the laundry, or working on your car. The benefits of this kind of praying are tremendous.

Five Scriptural Benefits of Praying in the Spirit

The following are five scriptural benefits of praying in the Spirit.

1. It builds you up (1 Cor. 14:4).
2. It stimulates your faith (Jude 20).
3. It helps you in your weaknesses (Rom. 8:26).
4. It brings rest and refreshing (Isa. 28:11–12).
5. It causes God to be made bigger in all you do (Acts 10:46).

You have just read about one of the success habits of uncommon achievers, and you may know from your own experience the powerful results that prayer produces. You may have heard the saying, "Little prayer, little power. Much prayer, much power. No prayer, no power." Developing a prayer habit is the foundation upon which everything else is built. Now go to it. Do not listen to the devil's lie that you are not worthy. Don't let him stop

> Little prayer, little power.
> Much prayer, much power.
> No prayer, no power.

you one second longer from praying. Hebrews 4:16 says we can approach God's throne boldly. Go to your Heavenly Father today. He is waiting for you. He wants to meet with you. He wants to show you "great and mighty things which you do not know" (Jer. 33:3).

Prayer opens the door for God to move in your life. Now open the door. Begin to take those small steps and start praying today. You will be excited when you begin to see the great things God will do as a result of your praying. Don't delay another day. Act now!

Take Action Now

I will develop the following prayer habits:

_____

_____

_____

_____

_____

_____

_____

_____

_____

_____

_____

_____

_____

_____

_____

_____

_____

_____

Specific things I will be praying for:

_____

_____

_____

_____

_____

_____

_____

_____

_____

_____

_____

_____

_____

_____

_____

_____

_____

_____

[i] *Merriam-Webster's Collegiate Dictionary*, 11th ed. (Springfield, Mass.: Merriam-Webster, Inc., 2003).

[ii] Albert Hibbert, *Smith Wigglesworth: The Secret of His Power* (Tulsa, Oklahoma: Harrison House, 1982), 44.

Create a Strong Spirit

The strong spirit of a man sustains him in bodily pain
or trouble, but a weak and broken spirit who
can raise up or bear?
—Proverbs 18:14 (*Amplified*)

Creating and developing a strong spirit is a key to overcoming obstacles in your life. If you have a strong spirit, you can walk in victory over anything that comes your way. The way you develop a strong spirit is by feeding your spirit on God's Word.

Put God's Word in Your Heart

JOHN 15:4

4 Abide in me, and I in you. As the branch cannot bear fruit of itself, except it abide in the vine; no more can ye, except ye abide in me.

Many people miss the part in this verse that refers to the Word of God *abiding* in them. For the Word—or anything else, for that matter—to *abide* in you, you must first be committed to it.

Some of the most successful ministers I know have read their Bible through more than 100 times. One of them has read his Bible from cover to cover more than 250 times. No wonder they're successful! God's Word is abiding in them. That type of investment in the Word has to produce a powerful anointing!

It's important to develop the habit of reading God's Word. Reading your Bible is vital to your spiritual growth. Job 23:12 says, "*. . . I have esteemed the words of his* [God's] *mouth more than my necessary food.*" Just like your body needs nourishment to be strong physically, your spirit man needs to be fed the Word of God in order to be strong spiritually. Jeremiah 15:16 says, "*Thy words were found, and I did eat them; and thy word was unto me the joy and rejoicing of mine heart. . . .*" God's Word will nourish your spirit

JOHN 15:7 (*NKJV*)

7 "If you abide in Me, and My words abide in you, you will ask what you desire, and it shall be done for you."

Notice the word *you* appears fives times in this verse. That means we have more to do with receiving from God than we even realize. We have to do the abiding.

We learn what rightfully belongs to us in Christ Jesus from the Bible. It is often referred to as God's Will and Testament. You know what a will is, don't you? It's a legal document people set up to make sure that, after they're gone, their heirs receive what belongs to them. This document details the person's instructions as to the distribution of his or her belongings.

The Bible illustrates God's will for our lives, and included in His will are many benefits, such as salvation, healing, joy, prosperity, protection . . . and the list goes on and on. There are many more blessings, and it's important to study God's Word to find out what truly belongs to us.

Sadly, too many people are living way below their rights and privileges that God has provided for them simply because they aren't aware of the blessings that are rightfully theirs. They don't know about all the good things Jesus left them in His will—the Bible.

It's Included in the Ticket

I'll never forget hearing the story of a man who worked for years to save money to go on a cruise. It was his lifelong dream to sail the ocean. After many years of hard work, he finally saved up enough money to buy a ticket to take a cruise.

After buying the ticket, the man realized that he didn't have enough money left over for food, so he filled his suitcases full of peanut butter and crackers to eat while he was at sea. During each mealtime, he would stand outside the dining room, looking in at all the people eating steak, lobster, incredible desserts, and so forth, and wishing he was in there eating too.

The last night of the cruise, the man happened to meet the captain of the ship. The captain asked him how he had enjoyed the food, bragging about the elaborate spread. Embarrassed, the passenger bowed his head, then looked up at the captain and said, "I didn't have enough money for the meals, only for the ticket."

Horrified, the captain exclaimed, "My dear sir! Didn't you know that the meals were included in the ticket price?"

This poor man could have partaken of all the delicious food, but instead he ate peanut butter and crackers in his cabin. Why? Because he didn't know what belonged to him.

A lot of Christians are the same way, living far below their rights and privileges in Christ simply because they do not know what belongs to them. As you read God's Word, you will find great and precious promises that belong to you.

'Can the Word'

When you continually put God's Word in you, it will come out when you need it most. Colossians 3:16 says, *"Let the word of Christ dwell in you richly . . . ."* Putting the Word in you is vitally important to creating and developing a strong spirit.

I like what one minister said about putting the Word in you. She referred to it as "canning the Word." It's like canning peaches. You put a lot of effort into picking and canning them in the summer when they're fresh. Then in the middle of winter you get to enjoy the fruits of your labor.

So it's important to "can the Word." Put it deep inside you, and then when you need it the most, it will bring you through any situation.

The Word in You Will
See You Through

Years ago I was the guest speaker at a church in a small town where there was no hotel, so I accepted an invitation to stay at the home of the associate pastor and his family.

This very nice and hospitable couple had several children who kept gerbils as pets. Each night after I had come home from preaching, as I lay in bed, I heard the little creatures going round and round in their little wheels. I thought to myself, *I'm sure glad they're in their cages . . . locked up . . . so there's nothing to worry about.*

While I was there, I was suddenly attacked with a terrible fever. Late that evening, after ministering, I returned to the pastor's home. I was completely exhausted and still fighting symptoms in my body.

I got into bed. Everyone else was sleeping. Suddenly I noticed the gerbils weren't making any of their usual noises. No wheels were turning! I thought, *Oh no. It's too quiet. Surely they can't be out of their cages!* I got out of bed, went into the room where the cages were kept, and sure enough, no gerbils! They were gone!

I thought, "I am not sleeping up here with gerbils running around everywhere!" So I—mighty woman of faith and power—grabbed a blanket and pillow, shut the upstairs doors and flew down the stairs to sleep on the couch, where there were no furry little gerbils on the loose . . . or so I thought.

I was so tired that I fell asleep immediately, but in the middle of the night I developed a high fever—so high that I started hallucinating. In this dreamlike state, I opened my eyes and there was a giant gerbil looming over me! Near the couch I was lying on was a large stereo with a huge speaker, and all of a sudden the stereo turned on!

I want to remind you here that none of this really happened. My fever-induced dream made me think that the stereo had started playing the song "By His Word." It goes, "By His Word, I have no fear in me. . . . By His Word, sickness can't dwell in me." It's a Word-filled song written by one of my friends.

Suddenly my fever broke and I snapped right out of that horrible dream completely healed! No more fever, flu symptoms, gerbils—real or imagined—and no stereo blaring out that music.

Through the years, I had listened to that song over and over. It is *filled* with the Word of God. I had put that song in me so much by listening to it so often that it was the only thing that *could* come out of me! You will manifest what you're full of. It was the Word abiding in me that set me free that night!

John 8:32 says, *"Ye shall know the truth, and the truth shall make you free."* When you deposit the Word in you, you'll be able to stand against the crisis of life when it comes! When you put God's Word in you, it will come out when you need it most.

The Law of Eventually

The law of eventually goes something like this: what you do daily determines what you become eventually.

Let's take our eating habits for example. Regardless of how painful it may be to admit this is true, your body is the direct result today of what you ate yesterday. If you like to eat pie, cookies, chocolate almond ice cream, and pizza on a somewhat regular basis, guess what? In most cases, you, as well as others, are going to be able to discern your eating habits from the outside! Why? Because you'll be wearing them!

I used to say that if I continue to eat all the things I like, *eventually* I will become a *big* evangelist! In other words, if you continue to eat too much, the law of eventually says that you're going to gain weight!

The Lord has shown me that I should never complain about what I permit. If I'm overweight, I shouldn't be complaining about it. Nobody put that food in my mouth except me!

Sacrificing what we want now for what we want to have *eventually* requires a combination of discipline and self-control. Neither of these qualities just drops on anyone!

Here's another example. I know a couple who sacrificed certain luxuries to save up money for a down payment on a bigger home. For two years, they didn't eat out very much at restaurants or buy a whole lot of new clothes. Now they have a big, beautiful, new home and it's not a strain on them financially. They're enjoying the fruits now because of the sacrifices they made in the past.

If you hang around successful people long enough, eventually their success can rub off on you. On the other hand, if you hang around lukewarm, non-dedicated people, eventually their ways can pull you down.

The same is true concerning spiritual things. If you spend time in the Word and go to church regularly, eventually you will grow spiritually and develop a strong spirit.

I realize we live in a fast-paced society, and you may be very busy. People want everything instantly. However, there are no "drive-through breakthroughs." Every person I know who devotes time and effort to daily prayer and study of the Word will tell you it's worth it. It pays off in the long run and you will love the results of developing a strong spirit.

Iron Sharpens Iron

Regular church attendance is vitally important to our spiritual growth. In church our spirit man is fed the Word of God. Not only that, it is very good for us to be in an atmosphere of faith with other believers. Proverbs 27:17 tells us that "iron sharpens iron." Something happens to you when you unite with other believers and you are worshiping the Lord together. Your spirit man is lifted and your emotions are ministered to as well.

By going to church regularly, you can make friends that will last a lifetime. It is important to have friends who believe the same way you do. They encourage your life. You may have heard the saying, "Show me who your friends are, and I'll show you who *you* are." One of the most important things you can do in developing a strong spirit is to surround yourself with positive people—people of like-precious faith.

God didn't create us to do things on our own. We need Him . . . and we need each other. Unfortunately, many of us Christians get so busy that we start to let church attendance slip. It's so easy to sleep in on Sunday, but if we will admit it, when we do get out of bed and make ourselves go to church, we feel so much better. We can leave the service feeling built up and better in general about life. If we want to see real success in our lives, we need to develop the habit of connecting with others.

Develop the Habit of Going to Church

LUKE 4:16

16 And he came to Nazareth, where he had been brought up: and, as his custom was, he went into the synagogue on the sabbath day, and stood up for to read.

Regular church attendance is a key to walking in victory. The verse above shows us that even Jesus had a custom, or habit, of going to the synagogue on the Sabbath day. The following scripture verses tell us that we should not forsake the assembling of ourselves together, meaning that we should not forsake going to church.

HEBREWS 10:24–25

24 And let us consider one another to provoke unto love and to good works:

25 Not forsaking the assembling of ourselves together, as the manner of some is; but exhorting one another: and so much the more, as ye see the day approaching.

We need to come together even more in these last days before Jesus returns. Yes, it's good to watch Christian TV and listen to tapes. But these should not replace our going to church; rather, they should add to it. There's nothing quite like being with other believers by regularly attending church.

Remember, what you do regularly determines what you become eventually. I am convinced that you cannot maintain a strong spirit and really walk in victory without developing the habit of fellowshipping with other believers on a regular basis.

Let's take a look at what the Bible says about fellowship.

ACTS 2:42

42 And they continued stedfastly in the apostles' doctrine and fellowship, and in breaking of bread, and in prayers.

Many times, the Early Church was so persecuted that they had to go to the extent of risking their lives just to meet together for church. Most Christians today don't have it that bad.

I remember preaching in Russia in one of the biggest churches in Moscow just after Communism fell. The pastors and believers were so thankful to God that they could now meet together in a huge arena without fear of what might happen to them.

The pastor, who had been in prison several times for preaching the Gospel, told me that they used to have to meet secretly in homes. They couldn't announce where they were going to meet for fear of being arrested, so each member had to seek God to find out where the meetings were going to be held each Sunday. He said it was amazing how God would speak to people and let them know where to meet for church. Now that's dedication! Some people I know won't go to church if it's raining or snowing!

Aren't you glad that you don't have to risk going to jail in order to attend church? But in America, many Christians still do not attend church faithfully. Church attendance polls have revealed that only one-third to one-sixth of the number of Americans who call themselves Christians attend church regularly.

You, as well as your children, will be tremendously edified and encouraged by the results that regular church attendance produces. Once you get in this wonderful habit of going to church consistently, your spirit man will be so edified that you will actually look forward to your next church service.

I wrote a book that I encourage you to read entitled *12 Ways to Be a Blessing to Your Church*. It is full of wonderful ideas on how to help your church and how to receive the most out of a church service. It also gives you tips on how to find the right church for you and your family. If you want your children to go to church, then you should set a good example for them to follow by going yourself.

Keep Your Spirit Man Strong

At the beginning of this chapter we read Proverbs 18:14, which indicated that a strong spirit will sustain you in any situation. In other words, if you continually develop the habit of keeping your spirit man strong, you will be able to overcome any attack that comes your way. A strong spirit can sustain you through the hard times that life may bring. Don't wait until trouble hits to get in the Word. Put God's

Word in you now and it will be there when you need it most. It's one of the success secrets of uncommon achievers.

Take Action Now

I will do the following things to keep my spirit strong:

HABIT #4

Practice Organization

For God is not a God of disorder but of peace.
—1 Corinthians 14:33 (*NIV*)

There are many benefits to practicing organization. It has actually been proven that keeping things clean and orderly in your life will create room for prosperity.

Look around your house. When you peek inside your pantry, do you hold tightly to the doorknob, guarding against injury from an avalanche of cereal boxes and canned goods? Or perhaps it's a closet door you dread opening. Maybe you can't stand the thought of cleaning out your refrigerator for fear of what might be growing in the container that's been left in there for several months.

Keeping Up With the Clutter

Someone once said that you can tell the state of a person's mind by looking at how clean his or her garage is. (Another person once asked, "Does that mean if I don't have a garage, I don't have a mind?")

One businessman I know, after interviewing a potential employee, asked to see the inside of his vehicle. He said if the applicant's car was a total mess and hadn't been cleaned in months, he wouldn't even consider hiring him. Wow!

One article on organization said that the average three-bedroom house contains approximately 350,000 items. However, you can turn a cluttered house into a house of order with just some determination, time, and effort. This may all seem overwhelming to you. How do you begin? One step at a time.

You may want to start with just one room. Professional organizers suggest that you begin by creating a list of what you would like to organize, such as important papers, bills, e-mail messages, dresser drawers, kitchen cupboards, or a linen closet. Then pick one category and concentrate on it. When you've finished with that category, then move on to the next one.

One thing you may want to do is buy some books on organization. I have read several books that have helped me to become more organized. Just recently I hired a professional organizer who came to my house and helped me put things in order.

I've read that one famous millionaire pays someone full time to do nothing but keep things clean and orderly around him. That employee keeps his boss's house and office clean, keeps his papers organized, and maintains order wherever he is. The millionaire says he thinks more clearly when things are well-organized. That organization helps create room for prosperity.

Good Habits Save Time

I remember once reading that the average person spends approximately six or seven hours a week looking for things he cannot find, such as important documents and car keys. That means the average person spends 312 hours a year looking for things he can't find. That's 13 full days—almost two entire weeks out of his life that is wasted because he isn't organized. Ouch!

If you will follow this simple plan, it will help you find things much quicker. It's called the "Everything Has a Home" plan, or EHAH, simply meaning that you should designate a home, space, or spot in which to keep each of your belongings.

For example, put your keys in the same place every time you walk in the door. One of my friends designates the outside pocket of her purse only for her keys. That way they are always readily accessible, because they're always in the same spot.

You may also want to designate a place for your television remote control. For example, you might always put it on top of the television when you're done using it. If everyone in the family knows where its "home" is, then you can find it a lot quicker when you need it.

In our ministry office, we designate a specific place for every item. This way, each employee knows exactly where to find each item. Have you ever spent hours looking for important documents such as your birth certificate, passport, or insurance papers? It would be a good idea for you to have some sort of a filing system to assign a home for these important documents. Your life will become much more productive as a result.

Inside and Out

Maybe the disorder in your house, office, car, or garage is an outward sign of what's going on inside you. Have you ever thought about that? Do you feel like a mess on the inside? Perhaps it's time to clean up some things, to get your life in order, inside and out. The longer you procrastinate, the harder it will be to make these improvements.

Getting organized may seem so overwhelming to you right now that you're not sure where to begin. Have you ever heard the saying, "How do you eat an elephant? One bite at a time." How do you tackle those piles of paper? One piece at a time! Just start somewhere.

I believe that if we are good stewards over the things the Lord has given us, then He can bless us with more. For example, the car you're driving right now might not be your ultimate dream car. However, if you will take good care of the one you have by keeping it clean, vacuumed, and well-maintained, I believe the Lord can bless you with something even better because you are being a good steward with what you have now. This has happened many times in my own life.

If you start taking care of things, you can create room for prosperity. And when God starts giving you the desires of your heart, you need to be grateful by being a good steward over them.

When I was attending Bible school, one of the ministers said something I've never forgotten. "We can tell," he said, "if you're going to make it in the ministry by looking in your dresser drawers."

I remember thinking, *Oh, dear God! I'm in big trouble.* So I went home and started cleaning! I said to myself, "Well, I'm not as organized as I want to be yet, but that doesn't mean I can't get there. I can change. I may not be perfect, but I can certainly make some changes at becoming better in this area than I am now."

None of the things I have shared are meant to condemn you, but rather to motivate you to live a more excellent life by developing the habit of organization.

Learn Time-Management Skills

In an effort to avoid feeling guilty, we Christians often say "yes" to everything that comes along. Being organized, operating out of a daily time-management notebook that anyone can find almost anywhere—even at a discount department store—will help you say "no" when you've already made time-consuming commitments elsewhere.

Some people think of time management as something that only business professionals need to do. That isn't true at all. Homemakers, teachers, employees, pastors, students, and those who don't even consider themselves to be a part of the professional marketplace still need to manage their time. Why? It helps them learn how to work smarter and not harder.

You can use well-developed organizational and time-management skills throughout your lifetime. They help you maintain good habits that can be applied to a variety of situations. These situations can involve very simple things like keeping your work space organized—whether it's a tool bench, your kitchen countertops, or your desk at home or the office. Use "input/output" trays or bins, and keep a notebook handy in order to jot down ideas and "to-do" items as they come to mind.

One business executive wrote down what he considered the top 15 time-wasters. Here is his list:

1. Telephone interruptions

2. Drop-in visitors

3. Meetings (scheduled and unscheduled)

4. Crises

5. Lack of objectives, priorities, and deadlines

6. Cluttered desk and personal disorganization

7. Ineffective delegation, and personal involvement in routine affairs and small details

8. Attempting too much at once, and unrealistic time estimates

9. Unclear chains of authority and responsibility

10. Inadequate, inaccurate, or delayed information

11. Indecision and procrastination

12. Lack of, or unclear, communication and instructions

13. Inability to say no

14. Lack of controls, standards, and progress reports to keep track of the completion of tasks

15. Fatigue and lack of self-discipline

At home, your list of the top five time-wasters might include the following items:

1. Watching too much television (It is said that the average American watches television 20 hours a week. That's nearly three hours a day!)

2. Talking on the phone too long

3. Unexpected visits from neighbors or family who stay too long

4. Lack of ability to stay focused on the task at hand (For example, you may be organizing your papers and come across some family photos. The next thing you know, you've spent several hours browsing through all your photo albums. You got sidetracked from your original goal. Ask me how I know . . .)

5. Not creating a list of items needed for a project, so that you have to run back and forth to the store to complete it.

I could add another item to the list immediately: hunting for misplaced things. What a time-waster! It would profit you to sit down and make your own list. This would give you a starting point for eliminating personal time-wasters. Time is very important!

The following is an eye-opening list of how much time the average person in the United States will spend on several common activities during a lifetime:

1. The average person will spend half a year waiting at red lights.

2. The average person will spend five years waiting in line.

3. The average person will spend six years eating.

4. The average person will spend two years playing phone tag.

5. The average person will spend one year just searching for lost things. [i]

Tips for Productive Time Management

Benjamin Franklin said, "Dost thou love life? Then do not squander time, for that is the stuff life is made of." Time is one way in which God has created us all equal. We all have 24 hours in a day. We each have 168 hours per week. It's how we *use* our time that matters most. Here are some tips for effective time management.

• **Get in the habit of making to-do lists.** Write down at least six things you want to accomplish each day. Before you go to the grocery store, create a list of items you need so that you don't forget them and waste time wandering the aisles.

• **Map out your errands in advance.** If you have several places to go, why not map out the order of your stops first? This will save you the time you'd lose backtracking or zigzagging from place to place.

• **Use a day planner or calendar.** A calendar is necessary to write down important appointments so that you won't forget them.

• **Try to keep all your addresses and phone numbers in one place.** Have you ever had more than one address book that you kept numbers in? It would be much more convenient to keep them all in one place. I use an electronic organizer that keeps all of my phone numbers, e-mail addresses, and other important information. It's so much easier just looking in one spot every time.

• **Plan your day.** Be sure to include time for interruptions—such as unexpected phone calls and drop-in visitors—and allow for some leisure time.

Develop a Savings Habit

Developing habits of organization, discipline, and self-control is especially important to your personal finances. Your financial state today is a result of your saving, giving, and spending habits yesterday. The law of eventually works here too (see Habit #3). Likewise, your financial future depends on the decisions you make today.

I once read about a librarian who made $10 an hour. Every month she faithfully put $100 into savings. Eventually she began to read books on investing and started directing her savings toward mutual funds and other slow-but-sure growth accounts.

Approximately 15 years later, she had over a half million dollars. When she was asked how she'd become such a wealthy librarian, she replied, "I just had a habit of investing $100 every month, no matter what!" That amounts to saving only about $3.33 every day.

Who wouldn't mind having an extra $10,000, $20,000, or $100,000? Well, to get there, start a new habit! Through patience—over time—you, too, can accumulate wealth.

Begin the habit of practicing organization. It's one of the success secrets of uncommon achievers.

Take Action Now

I will work on the following things to get more organized:

_____

_____

_____

_____

_____

_____

_____

_____

_____

_____

_____

_____

_____

[i] Bob Harrison, *Time Increase*, compact discs of messages (Tulsa: Harrison International, 2002).

HABIT #5
Take Control of Your Thought Life

For as he thinketh in his heart, so is he ....
—Proverbs 23:7

Did you know that you can change the direction of your life by changing your thoughts? Why? Because your life will go in the direction of your most dominant thoughts. The Apostle Paul said, *"Be renewed in the spirit of your mind; And ... put on the new man, which after God is created in righteousness and true holiness"* (Eph. 4:23–24).

The more your thinking changes for the better, the more successful your life is likely to be. Proverbs 23:7 says, *"For as he [a man] thinketh in his heart, so is he."* In other words, *you are what you think.*

Not long ago I read about a study that was done on the bumblebee. Did you know that, scientifically speaking, the bumblebee shouldn't be able to fly? It has been said that the weight of the bumblebee's body combined with its small wingspan makes it aerodynamically impossible for that little creature to get off the ground.

Some scientists will tell you beyond a shadow of a doubt that a bumblebee should not be able to fly. But somehow that bug takes off anyway! No one has ever told it that it couldn't. And do you know what? The bumblebee thinks it can. See—you are what you think you are. Unfortunately, so many Christians never become really successful because of the negative thoughts they believe to be true.

The Battle in Your Brain

I'll never forget a story I heard one pastor tell. He was driving home from work one afternoon when he heard an announcement over the radio. Authorities had issued a public alert that certain cans of tuna fish were contaminated. The announcer gave the brand information and the processing dates.

Then came the warning: "If you have eaten any of this particular tuna, you could die. Go to the hospital immediately."

Normally this would not have bothered the pastor because he almost never ate tuna. Unfortunately, it just so happened that for once his wife had made him—not one—but *two* tuna fish sandwiches for lunch, and he had eaten them both that very day!

The pastor started to worry. He worried and worried all the way home, and as soon as he got there he began digging through the garbage, looking for those tuna cans. Before long he found them, and sure enough . . . they were the exact same brand with the exact same dates the announcement had warned about. It was a match!

All of a sudden this pastor's mind started playing games with him. He saw himself lying in a casket. He began imagining his funeral. Quickly he ran to the mirror. After peering at himself for a while he started thinking, *You know, I don't feel very good.* The devil started telling him, "You're going to die. You ate that poisoned tuna. And you ate not one sandwich, but two!" His mind was bombarding him with fearful thoughts.

Expecting the worst, the pastor called the hospital to find out what symptoms he should look for, and they told him if nothing happened after 48 hours he would probably be fine. Well, that was the longest 48 hours of his life! The devil really played with his mind, but he never did get sick. He was fine!

This story just illustrates how we can fight a war in our heads. Our mind is the devil's favorite battlefield. Why? Because Satan knows how important our thought life is. He knows that if we have positive thoughts, full of the truth of the Word of God, then the sky is the limit!

So the devil attacks us in our thought life, telling us lie after lie. He does everything he can to cause us to worry. The devil knows the more you worry, the bigger your problem gets. Your problem may start out small, but if you don't get control of your thoughts, soon it will be huge, and it can defeat you.

The Power of Thoughts

There's another story I once heard that shows how powerful our thoughts can be. Two men decided they would catch a free ride by jumping onto a moving freight train. They thought it would be a thrill. As the train slowed down, they jumped aboard an empty boxcar and quickly shut the door. To their horror, as they pulled the door shut, it locked! They were locked in with no way out.

Then, just when they thought things couldn't get any worse, they discovered it was unusually cold in there. They were in a freezer car! There was frozen food all around them.

Panic rose in the mind of one of the men, as he imagined himself freezing to death in the boxcar. He even went so far as to scratch a good-bye note to his loved ones on the wall of the car with a rock: "I froze to death here."

But the other man wouldn't leave a good-bye note. In fact, he refused to, and he chastised his friend for thinking they were going to die.

Eventually, after many long hours, the train stopped and they were found. When the doors were opened, the man who had imagined himself freezing to death had died. The other one survived.

The ironic thing was that an autopsy was performed on the one who had died and they never could figure out what killed him. It wasn't cold enough in the boxcar for someone to freeze to death. He didn't die from the cold—the temperature wasn't low enough. He just *thought* he would die, and he did. That just goes to show how powerful our thoughts can be.

Think On These Things

You and I can walk in victory over the thoughts the devil sends against us as he tries to cause discouragement and defeat. Did you know that the number one battleground we face is in our minds? Our mind is the first place the enemy will attack us, and our mind is where the battle is either won or lost.

What we meditate on, and the things that we allow ourselves to think upon, will determine whether we stay down and discouraged or walk in victory. And God tells us what to think about in order to have that victory!

PHILIPPIANS 4:6–8 (*NIV*)

6 Do not be anxious about anything, but in everything, by prayer and petition, with thanksgiving, present your requests to God.

7 And the peace of God, which transcends all understanding, will guard your hearts and your minds in Christ Jesus.

8 Finally, brothers, whatever is true, whatever is noble, whatever is right, whatever is pure, whatever is lovely, whatever is admirable—if anything is excellent or praiseworthy—think about such things.

I believe with all my heart that many times we are our own worst enemy. There are a lot of people in the Church today who have what I call "stinkin' thinkin'". They always think the worst about every situation, when the Bible tells us to think the best. These "stinkin' thinkers" want to dwell on the worst possible outcome of every situation, so they're not disappointed if something goes wrong.

JOSHUA 1:8

8 This book of the law shall not depart out of thy mouth; but thou shalt meditate therein day and night, that thou mayest observe to do according to all that is written therein: for then thou shalt make

thy way prosperous, and then thou shalt have good
success.

Would you like to see your way made prosperous? Would
you like to have good success? God put the desire to be successful and prosperous in your heart. And He said that one
way you're going to make yourself prosperous and have
good success is by meditating in the Word of God day and
night so that you will remember it and do what it says. Why
not form the habit of meditating in God's Word day and
night? When you do, and when you put that Word into practice, the Bible says you will become a success.

The word *meditate* as it is used in Joshua 1:8 simply
means "to mutter." In other words, *to meditate* means to
mull something over, to think about it and speak it out loud
over and over.

To walk in vic-
tory, it is so helpful

> Miracles come in "cans."

to find a few scriptures and just meditate on them. Speak
them out of your mouth and get them down into your spirit.
A good one might be Philippians 4:13, which says, "I can do
all things through Christ who strengthens me" (*NKJV*).
Miracles come in cans—"I *can* do anything God has called
me to do, and I *can* be anything God has called me to be. I
can have everything God says I can have."

If You Can Conceive It,
You Can Receive It

When I was in high school, our girls' basketball team
won first place in our division. We were the best team

around. I really believe one of the reasons we were so good is that our coach had a rule that we could never say the words, "I can't." If you got caught saying those words at any time during the year, you had to run a mile.

I'll never forget the time my coach said to me, "Kate, I want you to slam-dunk it," and I said, "I can't." Then I ran a mile.

When I returned from my mile run in 85-degree weather, she said, "Kate, I want you to slam-dunk it," and I said, "Okay, I will!" Now of course since I am only 5 feet 4 inches tall, you might know that I never did slam-dunk it. But I sure did try!

Later I thought about ways I could have slammed it. I could have gotten a ladder, then climbed up and slammed it. In other words, there's always a way something can be done.

Can you imagine what it would be like if every time Christians said the words "I can't" they had to run a mile? Boy, would we all be in good shape! As a believer, you should never let the words "I can't" exist in your vocabulary. The Greater One lives in you, and you can do all things through Him.

One way to meditate on God's Word is just to lay in bed at night and think on a particular scripture. For example, if you've been battling fear in some area of your life, you might want to meditate upon Psalm 34:4, which says, *"I sought the Lord, and he heard me, and delivered me from all my fears."* How many of your fears? *All of them!* Continue to speak that Word out and just meditate on it over and over again, until it becomes reality in your life.

God says that when you do this—when you meditate on His Word—you're going to know what to do in life to cause your way to be prosperous, and you are going to have good success (Joshua 1:8).

Notice God said, "*You* will make your way prosperous." He didn't say, "*I'm* going to make your way prosperous." He said, "You will make your way prosperous by meditating in the Word—by keeping it in your heart and mouth—so that you can put that Word into practice. Developing the habit of meditating on God's Word and being a *doer* of that Word will bring victory to your life.

Super-Size It

A major trend in the fast-food industry these days is "super-sizing" your beverage or fries. We Americans like things big . . . the bigger, the better. Yet most Christians have a hard time seeing big things taking place in their lives, or they can't imagine God using them in a big way. But the fact of the matter is, God has big plans for your life. He wants you to think *big*! He has a super-size plan for you.

Ephesians 3:20 says, "[God] is able to do exceeding abundantly above all that we ask or think . . . ." Ask yourself what might be possible if you were to start super-sizing your thoughts. Now, I don't know about you, but I have a big imagination. God wants you to think big because He is a big God.

I remember when God started speaking to me about going on the radio. To me, that seemed big because I didn't have much money. God won't always call you to do something hard. Sometimes He will call you to do something impossible!

If your dream is so small that you don't need God to pull it off, then it's probably not of Him. You need a God-size dream! What I mean by that is, your dream and vision should be so big that if God doesn't get involved in it, you will fail.

Expect the Favor of God

So many people have experienced rejection. They go through life thinking everyone is going to reject them. Maybe they experienced a lot of unhappiness in their childhood, and so they just automatically think that people will not like them.

And what happens? People don't like them, and people reject them. Why? Because they already think that way about themselves. They think thoughts such as, *I am no good, I always mess up, I am lazy,* or *I'm always blowing it.* They have a bad self-image, and it projects out to other people who in turn just reflect back what they see. Remember—you are what you think you are.

I know a lot of people who automatically expect others not to like them before they even meet them. We need to change our thinking to believe the best. When thoughts of rejection come, do what Second Corinthians 10:5 says and take those thoughts captive. Don't let them take you captive. That scripture also says we are to cast down imaginations. Don't let those negative imaginations cast *you* down.

Program a New Habit

We need to reprogram our thinking . . . and program a new habit. I do some of my work on computers now. But there was a time when I first started learning the computer that I wanted to throw it out the window. I would feel like screaming, "Get rid of this thing!"

But eventually I learned my way around a laptop. I discovered that sometimes you have to change a file or change a program. Many times when you add new software you need to get rid of other stuff that's on the hard drive because it is taking up too much room and using up too much memory.

In the same way, God says we are to renew our mind.

ROMANS 12:2

2 And be not conformed to this world: but be ye transformed by the renewing of your mind . . . .

Our mind is to be renewed or transformed through the Word of God. We need to reprogram our mind to think in line with and according to the Word of God. We need to take out the old and put in the new.

In other words, we need to go into the computer of our mind and wipe out the old negative, wrong, stinkin' thinkin' and reprogram it with what the Bible says is true.

Maybe you've been trained to think wrong. But I encourage you now to begin to reprogram your mind. Every time you're faced with a situation, ask yourself, "What does the Bible say? What does the Word of God say concerning this?" That's the only way to take control of your thoughts and reprogram your thinking.

The Bible says that the Holy Spirit will show you things to come (John 16:13) and bring all things to your remembrance (John 14:26). But He can't bring anything to your remembrance that you haven't put in there yet! He can't bring scriptures to your remembrance if you've never put any in you.

That's why it's important that you hear the Word, go to a good church, and listen to good teaching tapes and good radio programs. If you put the Word in your heart, then in your time of need the Holy Spirit will bring that Word to your mind and to your heart.

Your life can change dramatically if you make a habit of meditating on the Word and taking captive all the negative and destructive thoughts that the devil brings against you. As you replace negative thoughts with God's thoughts and put the Word deep into your heart, you can reap a great reward!

Whether or not we have joy in our lives is a direct result of taking control of our thought life. The writer in Acts 26:2 said, "I think myself happy." If he can do this, then so can we. Joy is a decision. Don't allow thoughts of discouragement to stay! Isaiah 26:3 says, *"Thou wilt keep him in perfect peace, whose mind is stayed on thee: because he trusteth in thee."* Get in the habit of thinking on good things. It's one of the success secrets of uncommon achievers!

Take Action Now

Some thinking I want to reprogram:

_____

_____

_____

_____

_____

_____

_____

_____

_____

Scriptures to meditate on in order to renew my thinking:

_____

_____

_____

_____

_____

_____

_____

_____

_____

_____

HABIT #6

Cultivate the Power of
Positive Confession

Death and life are in the power of the tongue . . . .
—Proverbs 18:21

*Through faith we understand that the worlds were framed
by the word of God . . . .*
—Hebrews 11:3

The above scriptures reveal that there is tremendous power
in words. God Himself framed the world we live in by the
words that He spoke. In the Book of Genesis He said, "Let
there be light," and there was. The Bible tells us in Ephesians
5:1 that we are to be imitators of God (*NKJV*). We need to
talk like God. There literally is a miracle in your mouth!

Talk Your Way to Victory

I'll never forget the time the Lord said to me, "Kate, you
can talk yourself into anything." What He meant by that was
that I can talk my way into health, healing, strength, wisdom, prosperity, or whatever else I need by releasing my
faith with words.

Romans 10:17 tells us that faith comes by hearing the Word of God. However, it's not enough just to hear the Word; we must *act on* what we hear. We must release our faith. How do we do that? With our words.

One time I was watching a television interview with an awesome minister of God. One of the men sitting there during the interview turned to the minister and said, "Brother, I've got a lot of faith." The minister's reply hit me right between the eyes. He said, "Well, brother, that's your problem. You've still got it! You have to *release* your faith."

Another minister illustrated it this way: It's possible for a person to actually starve to death with money in his pocket. In order not to starve, that person must go to the store and release his money so he can buy something to eat. He must turn his money loose for it to help him.

You and I must do exactly the same thing with our faith. We must release it

> Faith is released when we speak . . . God's Word.

and turn our faith loose. Faith is released when we speak in line with God's Word. Let's look at a powerful example of this in Mark's Gospel.

MARK 5:25–34

25 And a certain woman, which had an issue of blood twelve years,

26 And had suffered many things of many physicians, and had spent all that she had, and was nothing bettered, but rather grew worse,

27 When she had heard of Jesus, came in the press behind, and touched his garment.

28 For she said, If I may touch but his clothes, I shall be whole.

29 And straightway the fountain of her blood was dried up; and she felt in her body that she was healed of that plague.

30 And Jesus, immediately knowing in himself that virtue had gone out of him, turned him about in the press, and said, Who touched my clothes?

31 And his disciples said unto him, Thou seest the multitude thronging thee, and sayest thou, Who touched me?

32 And he looked round about to see her that had done this thing.

33 But the woman fearing and trembling, knowing what was done in her, came and fell down before him, and told him all the truth.

34 And he said unto her, Daughter, thy faith hath made thee whole; go in peace, and be whole of thy plague.

Notice in verse 34 that Jesus said *her faith* made her whole. If this woman's faith could make her whole, then your faith can make you whole! Why? Because Jesus is the same yesterday, today, and forever (Heb. 13:8).

Three powerful things happened that brought about this woman's miracle. As we read other accounts throughout the New Testament, we see the same three things taking place to bring healing and deliverance to the lives of people.

1. *Hearing.* Verse 27 says she *heard* of Jesus. (And according to Romans 10:17, faith comes by hearing.)

2. *Believing.* She believed what she heard about Jesus. *Decide right now to believe God's Word.*

3. *Acting.* She acted. *The number one way to act on God's Word is to say something.* Verse 28 tells us, *"For she SAID, If I may touch but his clothes, I shall be whole."*

In Luke chapter 6, we see the exact same three things happening. A multitude of people heard Jesus preach. They believed what they heard, they acted on the Word, and then they received their miracle.

LUKE 6:17–19

17 And he came down with them, and stood in the plain, and the company of his disciples, and a great multitude of people out of all Judaea and Jerusalem, and from the sea coast of Tyre and Sidon, which came to hear him, and to be healed of their diseases;

18 And they that were vexed with unclean spirits: and they were healed.

19 And the whole multitude sought to touch him: for there went virtue out of him, and healed them all.

Notice it says that He healed them *all*! This passage of Scripture gives us more evidence that *hearing, believing,* and *acting* equals *receiving.*

Here we go again! In Acts 14:7–10 we see another powerful account of these same principles at work in the life of a man who was paralyzed.

ACTS 14:7–10

7 And there they preached the gospel.

8 And there sat a certain man at Lystra, impotent in his feet, being a cripple from his mother's womb, who never had walked:

9 The same heard Paul speak: who stedfastly beholding him, and perceiving that he had faith to be healed,

10 Said with a loud voice, Stand upright on thy feet. And he leaped and walked.

This crippled man did exactly the same three things as the woman with the issue of blood and the multitude of people did, and he received his miracle. However, in this account, Jesus was not the one preaching; Paul was. It really doesn't matter who is preaching as long as it's the Word of God being preached, and we who are exposed to that Word are hearing it, believing it, and acting on it.

The people in all three of these New Testament accounts received their miracle by doing these three things. God is no respecter of persons (Acts 10:34). If we will do these same three things, we can receive our miracle too.

Healed of Lupus

I've seen these three principles work in the lives of people I know personally. One morning, my phone rang, and a relative on the other end said, "Kate, I've just been to the doctor and the diagnosis isn't good. He said I have lupus." But then she said, "This is no surprise to God—it's easy for Him to heal lupus!"

How true that is. Lupus is just a name, and the Name of Jesus is above the name of lupus. The Name of Jesus is above the name of cancer, arthritis, diabetes, heart disease, ADD, bipolar disorder, panic attacks, depression, or whatever problem you may be dealing with.

My relative called me on a Friday and was planning on attending a meeting I was ministering at the following Tuesday. She was coming to have hands laid on her for healing. The Lord put it on my heart to share with her the account we read earlier in Mark chapter 5 about the woman with the issue of blood. I especially emphasized verse 28 from *The Amplified Bible*, which reads, "For she *kept saying*, If I only touch His garments, I shall be restored to health."

To "keep saying" means exactly that—you keep saying something. What did the woman with the issue of blood keep saying? She kept saying, "When I touch His garment, I'll be healed." This woman released her faith with words.

I encouraged my relative to follow this woman's example. She agreed that she would release her faith between Friday and Tuesday by saying, "When hands are laid on me Tuesday, I'll be healed of lupus."

Boy, did she act on the Word! She said it continually. She said it when she got up in the morning and all through the day. She called me on the phone several times and said, "Kate! Just thought I'd call and tell you that I'm coming to your meeting Tuesday, and when hands are laid on me, I'll be healed of lupus."

She then called my mother on the phone and said, "Guess what? I'm going to Kate's meeting on Tuesday and when hands are laid on me, I'll be healed of lupus."

She was shopping at the mall and bumped into a friend and said, "Hey! I'm going to a meeting Tuesday. And when hands are laid on me, I'll be healed of lupus."

By the time Tuesday rolled around, she had released her faith so many times that she was ready. She really got herself into position to receive from God.

As soon as I finished preaching, she came forward to have hands laid on her. As we were about to pray, she stopped me and said, "Kate, I just want to say it *one more time.* When you lay hands on me right now, I believe the power of God is going to flow into my body and I'll be healed of lupus!"

I laid hands on her, and guess what happened? Nothing! Nothing in the natural, that is. She didn't feel anything; she didn't fall or even feel a goose bump. A glory ball didn't roll in the back door and hit her upside the head.

After we prayed, she said, "Kate, does it still work even though I didn't fall or feel anything?" I told her, "Absolutely!" She said, "Thanks, that's all I needed to know. I'm now healed of lupus. Thank You, Jesus!" Then she went back to her seat.

The next morning, she woke up feeling a little bit better, and she was still praising God that she was healed of lupus. The following day, she felt even better. By the end of the week, she felt so good that she made a doctor's appointment. Boy, I like that! She made a feel-good doctor's appointment! What is a feel-good doctor's appointment? It's, "I feel so good, I think I'll go to the doctor!"

Well, she did. After running a bunch of tests on her, the doctor came back and said, "We don't know what happened, but you don't have lupus anymore."

She replied, "I'll tell you exactly what happened. I went to a meeting Tuesday and had hands laid upon me, and when I did, the power of God flowed into my body and I was healed of lupus!"

Her faith worked today just like the faith of that woman with the issue of blood worked in Bible days. She talked her way to victory. Her faith made her whole, and your faith can make you whole as well.

You too can talk your way to victory! We must get in the habit of speaking faith-filled words on a daily basis. For example, every day of my life I confess, "I have favor with God and man." Guess what? It works! I truly have favor everywhere I go. Why is that? Because I speak it daily.

Call Those Things Which Be Not as Though They Were

ROMANS 4:17

17 . . . God, who quickeneth the dead, and calleth those things which be not as though they were.

God Himself is in the habit of calling those things that be not as though they were. He is not the only one who has done this. Abraham did it too.

When you look up this word *calleth*, it literally means "to summon." Have you ever been summoned to court? What does that mean? It means you have to appear—you don't have a choice. When you and I call those things that be not as though they were, those things that we call for have to appear. They *must* show up; they don't have a choice.

Joel 3:10 says, ". . . *let the weak say, I am strong.*" Why did God tell the weak person to say, "I am strong"? Because that person will have exactly what they say. They will be strong.

I remember hearing an awesome testimony about a woman who had stomach cancer. She had lost a lot of weight and couldn't eat—she was incredibly weak. A minister went to pray for her and got her to act on Joel 3:10 by confessing "I am strong" several times a day.

Gradually this woman started gaining strength and then got her appetite back. After a period of time, she gained all her weight back and was completely healed of stomach cancer!

Proverbs 18:21 says, *"Death and life are in the power of the tongue. . . ."* This woman received her healing as a result of calling those things that be not as though they were.

Delivered From Addiction

This principle of calling those things that be not as though they were will work in every area of your life. A friend of mine shared a powerful story with me of how she was delivered from smoking. She had smoked several packs a day for many years. After becoming a Christian, she really wanted to please God and break this bad habit.

My friend tried everything in the natural to quit, and nothing was working. She became extremely discouraged and felt condemned until she heard a sermon on calling those things that be not as though they were. She realized that she had an even worse habit than smoking, and that was the habit of constantly saying, "I can't quit. It's so hard to stop smoking."

The Lord revealed to her that she was defeated because of the negative words she was speaking. Proverbs 6:2 says we are snared by the words of our mouth. She decided she was going to act on the Word of God by changing what she said. She got in the habit of confessing daily, "I am a non-smoker."

She kept on saying, "I am a non-smoker," even though she was still smoking. Even in between puffs, she still called those things that be not as though they were. She continued to do this day after day.

One morning she woke up and went to reach for her pack of cigarettes, as she had done every morning for many years. Suddenly it hit her and she thought, "Wait a minute! I don't need to smoke those. I'm a non-smoker!" She never smoked another cigarette again. She was completely delivered!

After seeing this principle from the Word of God work in such a powerful way, my friend realized that if "calling those things that be not as though they were" could deliver her from smoking, then it could also work in bringing healing to her body. She'd had diabetes for many years and had to take insulin shots every day.

My friend began to apply this same habit of "calling things that be not as though they were" where her diabetes was concerned. Every day she would call her body healed. Now she didn't throw away her medicine, but every time she had to take a shot, she would say, "Thank You, Lord, for healing me. I believe I am no longer a diabetic. I call my body healed."

Some time passed and nothing appeared to have changed, but she did not allow it to discourage her. Listen friend, don't allow the devil to discourage you just because some time has passed and you don't see any change! Galatians 6:9 says you will reap if you don't give up.

So don't faint in your confession of faith. The Bible says it will come to pass. Hebrews 10:23 says, *"Let us hold fast the profession of our faith without wavering; (for he is faithful that promised.)"* The word *profession* actually means "confession." Another verse in Hebrews also tells us to hold fast to our confession.

HEBREWS 4:14
14 Seeing then that we have a great high priest, that is passed into the heavens, Jesus the Son of God, let us hold fast our profession.

My friend continued calling herself healed of diabetes. However, one day she felt terribly sick and had to be rushed to the emergency room. After running a series of tests, the doctors informed her that the reason she was so sick was that she had been taking insulin for diabetes, and their tests showed that she was not a diabetic! Praise God! Calling those things that be not as though they were really worked for her and it can work for you too!

The Habit of Speaking Right

The great news is, the Word of God can work for you, too, when you speak it. Can you think of some areas in your life that you need to speak the Word of God over? Get in the habit of speaking positive words rather than negative ones.

Sometimes we say negative things that we don't even mean simply out of habit. For example, you may say, "These kids are driving me crazy," or "My back is killing me," or "I'm a fat cow; I can't lose weight; It's just so hard," or "I'm broke," or "I can't afford that," or "Boy, am I tired!"

Sometimes just making a little adjustment in what we say can bring big-time breakthroughs. There are some clear instructions concerning this in Malachi chapter 3. This passage applies to money, and God promised He would pour out blessing to those who act on His Word by tithing and giving.

MALACHI 3:10–14

10 Bring ye all the tithes into the storehouse, that there may be meat in mine house, and prove me now herewith, saith the Lord of hosts, if I will not open you the windows of heaven, and pour you out a blessing, that there shall not be room enough to receive it.

11 And I will rebuke the devourer for your sakes, and he shall not destroy the fruits of your ground; neither shall your vine cast her fruit before the time in the field, saith the Lord of hosts.

12 And all nations shall call you blessed: for ye shall be a delightsome land, saith the Lord of hosts.

13 YOUR WORDS HAVE BEEN STOUT AGAINST ME, saith the Lord. Yet ye say, What have we spoken so much against thee?

14 Ye have said, It is vain to serve God: and what profit is it that we have kept his ordinance, and that

we have walked mournfully before the Lord of hosts?

These verses speak of a group of people who were tithing and giving. However, they weren't getting much in return—it wasn't working. They wanted to know why it wasn't working. So in verse 13, God told them why. He said that their words were stout against Him. I like to say it this way: their words were *doubt* against Him.

What these people were doing was giving their offerings but then going home and saying, "It's not working." The Lord told them it wasn't working because they kept saying, "It's not working." What a powerful revelation! It is important that we speak right words. Faith words.

Maybe you are giving and yet you have been saying, "I don't understand why it's not working." That's exactly what these people were doing.

As a believer, you should never say the words "I can't," because as I said earlier, miracles come in "cans." "I *can* do all things through Christ who strengthens me" (Phil. 4:13 *NKJV*). Decide today that you will never again say the words "I can't" or "I can't afford it." You may need to say, "I choose not to purchase that right now."

I want to encourage you to stop right now and say out loud, "I give, and it comes back to me—good measure, pressed down, shaken together, and running over according to Luke 6:38. The Word is working for me. I'll never be broke another day in my life. This is the poorest I'll ever be. I am blessed!"

You Can Have What You Say

MARK 11:23

23 For verily I say unto you, That whosoever shall say unto this mountain, Be thou removed, and be thou cast into the sea; and shall not doubt in his heart, but shall believe that those things which he saith shall come to pass; HE SHALL HAVE WHAT-SOEVER HE SAITH.

Jesus said we can have what we say. You may know some people who make fun of this. But don't you worry about them—you just keep on being blessed for being a doer of the Word.

I heard a story about one man who said, "That Mark 11:23 stuff doesn't work. You can't have what you say. I never have what I say." It worked for him all right! He got exactly what he said he would get—nothing!

Having what you say works in the little things too. One time someone told me they thought it was silly to believe God for front row parking spots. He said, "You can't do that!" I said, "Well, it works for me. I always get the front row parking spots." I told him he could just keep parking in the back of the lot, and I'll just keep parking in the front. He has what he says, and I have what I say!

The Lord dealt with one pastor I know concerning the words he was speaking over his church. Anytime someone would ask him about the size of his church, he was in the habit of saying, "We're just a small church." The Lord revealed to him that if he kept on calling it small, then it would stay small.

So he changed his confession. He started saying, "We're a growing church. We are reaching and helping lots of people." Before long, his church starting growing and reaching more people.

Because I Say So

JOB 22:28

28 Thou shalt also decree a thing, and it shall be established unto thee: and the light shall shine upon thy ways.

To decree a thing actually means "to speak, say, or declare a thing." If there are some areas in your life that need changing, begin a habit of saying what you want to see, even in the little areas.

I know one woman who struggled with her weight and began confessing, "I weigh 135 pounds. I love to exercise and eat healthy. I am disciplined and maintain a healthy lifestyle." It worked for her. She lost weight and got down to 135 pounds.

Begin the habit of making some of the following confessions:

- I always have more than enough.
- I have favor with God and man.
- Everything I put my hand to prospers.
- Every sickness, virus, disease, or germ that touches my body dies instantly in the Name of Jesus.

- I am the head and not the tail, above only and not beneath.
- I am strong and I am rich.
- I am the righteousness of God in Christ.
- I am forgiven.
- All my needs are met and money comes to me in abundance.

Hearken to the Voice of God's Word

HEBREWS 1:13–14

13 But to which of the angels said he at any time, Sit on my right hand, until I make thine enemies thy footstool?

14 Are they not all ministering spirits, sent forth to minister for them who shall be heirs of salvation?

The Bible says that we have ministering angels who assist us here on the earth. They have been sent forth to minister for us. We know that they protect us (Ps. 91:11). But they also have a part to play in our prosperity. Let me show you that according to the Scriptures:

PSALM 103:20–21

20 Bless the Lord, ye his angels, that excel in strength, that do his commandments, hearkening unto the voice of his word.

21 Bless ye the Lord, all ye his hosts; ye ministers of his, that do his pleasure.

Verse 21 tells us that the angels do God's pleasure. What does God take pleasure in? Prospering you! Psalm 35:27 says, ". . . 'Let the Lord be magnified, Who has pleasure in the prosperity of His servant' " (*NKJV*). Psalm 23:1 says, *"The Lord is my shepherd; I shall not want."* Psalm 34:10 says, *"The young lions do lack, and suffer hunger: but they that seek the Lord shall not want any good thing."*

We see that angels can assist us where our money is concerned. How do we get our angels working on our behalf? Psalm 103:20 tells us that they hearken to the voice of God's Word. That means we need to be speaking faith-filled words. If you're not speaking the Word, then your angels are not hearkening. No Word, no hearkening. Speak the Word and your angels get moving.

A close minister friend of mine shared a dream with me that she believes came from the Lord. She had been standing in faith for quite some time believing God for a certain thing. In the dream, she saw an angel leave Heaven with a big package wrapped up in a box with a ribbon. This represented her answer.

As my minister friend praised and worshipped God for the answer to her prayer, the angel carrying the package seemed to speed up on his trip down to earth. As time passed, she started to get discouraged and began speaking negative words. She started to say, "I guess the Word isn't working."

As my friend continued to speak negative words in her dream, she noticed that the angel heard the words of doubt and unbelief coming out of her mouth and stopped right above her house. The angel had a very sad look on his face, and he headed back up to Heaven with her package.

The Lord revealed to my friend how close her answer was and what happened when she started to speak negative words. As soon as she changed her confession and started praising God again, the angel perked up and was able to zoom back down to the earth with her answer! As she opened her package, the angel was filled with joy.

Of course, we don't base our believing on someone's dreams or visions, but this illustrates an important point, and my friend did get her breakthrough when she changed her confession.

The Angel Came for Faith-Filled Words

Daniel experienced in real life something similar to my friend's dream. In the Book of Daniel, chapter 10, Daniel was praying and a battle was going on. The devil was fighting to try and stop his answer from coming. The scripture says there was a war that went on in the heavenlies for 21 days (v. 13). The devil tried to stop Daniel's prayers from being answered, but he could not prevail.

After 21 days, an angel appeared to Daniel and spoke some powerful things to him. First of all he said that Daniel's words were heard from the first day he prayed. Then the angel said to Daniel, ". . . I have come because of your words" (v. 12 *NKJV*). Wow! The angel came because of words that Daniel spoke. The angels do hearken to God's Word. I believe Daniel spoke faith words.

Are your angels unemployed? Or have you been keeping them busy by speaking faith-filled words?

Wouldn't it be amazing if we could see into the realm of the spirit? You might look at one Christian and see his angel and hear that angel say, "Boy, this guy is boring. He never gives me anything to do."

Then you might look at another believer and hear his angel say, "Man, this guy keeps me busy! He's got me bringing in his money, protecting his children, and doing a lot of other things for him. He's putting me to work!"

Angelic Intervention

From the time my mom got saved, she would always pray and plead the blood of Jesus over all of us kids and claim God's angelic protection over us. She used to be a world champion worrier until she got delivered and began to confess that God's angels had charge over her family.

I'll never forget the time I experienced God's supernatural protection firsthand. I was 16 years old and went snow skiing with some friends. I was just a beginner and got talked into going down one of the big hills.

As I started sliding down the hill, I discovered I had made a huge mistake. I began to pick up speed and could not slow myself down. I tried everything, including going side to side, but nothing was working. Instead, I started building momentum and was suddenly going super fast down the mountain.

Not too far in front of me was a huge tree and my ski was stuck in a rut. I was headed right for the tree. I tried turning, but to no avail. Then I tried with all my might just to wipe out before I hit it. I figured the wipeout would hurt, but not as bad as smacking into this tree at who-knows-how-many miles per hour. But I couldn't even fall down. I just kept going faster!

I literally thought I was going to die. I began to call on the Name of Jesus. My friend, who was skiing right behind me, was petrified, yelling and screaming, knowing the danger that was ahead of me.

I was just about to crash right into the tree when suddenly I felt a Being literally *pick me up in the air*, move me over to the side of the tree, and set me down softly in the snow. The only way I can describe it is that I felt as light as a feather floating to the ground.

I didn't say a word to my friend who was behind me, but he saw the whole thing. He said, "Kate, I saw you get lifted up in the air, and then you floated over to the side of the tree and slowly and gently sat on the ground." He was absolutely in awe of what that angel did. He still talks about it to this day.

I am so glad that I had a praying mother who believed in the power of the blood of Jesus and in divine angelic protection. And you have protection too!

Take Hold of the Reins of Your Life

JAMES 3:2–4

2 For in many things we offend all. If any man offend not in word, the same is a perfect man, and able also to bridle the whole body.

3 Behold, we put bits in the horses' mouths, that they may obey us; and we turn about their whole body.

4 Behold also the ships, which though they be so great, and are driven of fierce winds, yet are they turned about with a very small helm, whithersoever the governor listeth.

The preceding verses reveal to us that our words steer our life in the direction we want it to go. Verse 4 says our words are like a rudder on a ship. What is a rudder designed to do? It determines which way the ship will go.

Verse 3 talks about putting a bit in a horse's mouth. What is that bit designed to do? If you've ever been horseback riding, then you know that if you pull on the reins to the right, the horse should go to the right. (That's true unless you're like me and you don't ride horses much.)

One time I got talked into horseback riding. Having almost no riding experience, I didn't catch on when they told me this horse had not been ridden in over a year. They assured me it would be okay. I was hoping the horse was at least 40 or 50 years old, but this was not the case.

As soon as I got on the horse, it took off faster than a speeding bullet! It took off before I could grab the reins. As we went galloping down a dirt road, the reins were dragging on the ground.

Then the horse hit me in the head with its head several times, trying to get rid of me. I was yelling for it to slow down, but "whoa horsy" wasn't doing the trick. I thought about jumping, but the ground was going by too fast.

Ahead of me I spotted a stop sign, and the horse ran right through it. Pretty soon I saw another stop sign approaching, but this time a major highway was ahead of me with lots of cars speeding by.

The good news is, my horse finally got tired and slowed down enough for me to jump off before we reached the intersection. We were both fine, except that I'm sure we both needed healing for headaches!

I learned a valuable lesson that day. If you don't have hold of the reins, your horse will run in any old direction it wants to, and you will have absolutely no control over it. Likewise, the Book of James says that you must take hold of the reins of your life, which are the words you speak daily.

Your Mountain Needs to Hear Your Voice

Often, thoughts of fear or doubt will enter your mind. Jesus gave us a powerful tool to come against the devil and thoughts of fear, and that tool is speaking words.

Your words are more powerful than thoughts. Each time the devil tempted Jesus in the wilderness, He resisted him by saying, "It is written" (Matt. 4:4–10). When He did, the devil had to flee. Jesus could have just thought, *It is written,* but instead, He spoke it. I believe He did that to show you and me the power in the words we speak.

In Mark chapter 11 Jesus spoke to the fig tree. The passage says that the disciples heard it, so we know for sure that Jesus spoke out loud. The minute He spoke the command of faith, the power of God went into action and began working on that tree.

The very next day they saw the results of what Jesus had said. What He had said had come to pass.

Jesus then went on in verse 22 to tell us how our faith works. He instructed His disciples to *have faith in God.* A marginal note in my Bible says that those words could also be translated, *"have the faith of God."* Then, in verse 23, Jesus told us what the faith of God, or the God-kind of faith, is.

MARK 11:23

23 For verily I say unto you, That whosoever shall say unto this mountain, Be thou removed, and be thou cast into the sea; and shall not doubt in his heart, but shall believe that those things which he saith shall come to pass; HE SHALL HAVE WHAT-SOEVER HE SAITH.

Notice that Jesus said, *". . . whosoever . . . shall have whatsoever HE saith."* Three times in this one verse, Jesus mentions *saying* something. That means we must do a whole lot of "saying" or speaking to our mountains!

Did you know that money has ears? So do tumors! What I mean by that is, they have to listen to you when you speak. If you curse a tumor and command it to shrivel up and die, it must listen to you and obey you. When you call in a buyer for a house you may need to sell, someone has to show up. You say, "House, I call you sold in the Name of Jesus!"

Why not call your car paid for? One time I said to my car, "Car, you may think you are a Chrysler, but I now call you a 'paid for.'" Every time I got in my car, I called it paid for. It wasn't long before it was completely paid off, years ahead of time!

You can do this too. It really does work. One friend of mine called her backslidden daughter home every day. She'd call her name and say, "Cheryl, I call you home to Jesus." The daughter was out at the bars all the time, but that didn't stop her mom from calling her home. She even started dating a guy she met at the bar, and things were looking worse. Then the two of them got married.

But my friend kept calling her daughter back into the family of God, and God moved in an awesome way. The daughter's husband was gloriously saved and filled with the Holy Spirit. He felt called to preach, so he went to Bible school for two years to train for the ministry! My friend's daughter came back to the Lord and is preparing for ministry to help assist her husband.

Begin the habit today of speaking faith-filled words over yourself and your family. There is a miracle in your mouth. Your mountain needs to hear your voice, so start speaking God's Word today.

Speaking faith-filled words is the golden key that unlocks the supernatural flow of God's power in our life. It's a daily habit of uncommon achievers.

Take Action Now

Build your own faith confession here, based on the Word of God.

Examples: *I have favor with God and man* (Ps. 5:12).

All my needs are met (Phil. 4:19).

I call my body healed (1 Peter 2:24).

I am strong (Joel 3:10).

_____

_____

_____

_____

_____

_____

_____

_____

_____

_____

_____

_____

_____

_____

_____

_____

_____

HABIT #7

Grow in Your Love Walk

I have had the awesome privilege of meeting some of the world's greatest ministers of the Gospel, and I have thought things like, *Wow, their faith walk must be tremendous.* And that was true.

However, it wasn't their faith walk alone that made them so successful. I came to find out that it was their love walk that really put them over.

The habit of walking in love is probably the most important spiritual fruit that can be developed in order to live a victorious Christian life. Why is this? Because love never fails (1 Cor. 13:8). As you walk in love, you cannot fail!

In the Old Testament God gave Moses the Ten Commandments. However, in the New Testament Jesus gave us a new commandment.

JOHN 13:34

34 A new commandment I give unto you, That ye love one another; as I have loved you, that ye also love one another.

When you walk in this new commandment, the law of love, you're going to be fulfilling the Ten Commandments, because if you love your neighbor you're not going to steal from them. If you love someone, you're not going to kill them, covet their belongings, or do anything else to harm them.

I'll be honest with you: it takes work to develop your love walk. But we know that love is a fruit of the Spirit, and you can grow in this fruit of love. It is important to know that if you have been born again, then God's love is already abiding in you.

ROMANS 5:5

5 . . . the love of God is shed abroad in our hearts by the Holy Ghost which is given unto us.

As a Christian, you have God's love in your heart. When you were born again, you received God's love nature. His love is a part of you. You *do* have love for others, even people who have treated you badly. Now mind you, sometimes you have to stir up that love.

Let's take a minute and talk about what love is *not*. For one thing, love is *not* a feeling. Often the devil will make you feel as though you're not walking in love if you're not experiencing "ooey-gooey," mushy love-feelings toward someone.

But we must realize that love is a decision, not a feeling. By faith, we must decide to release God's love and forgiveness toward those who have hurt us or done us wrong.

Jesus told us that, in order for our prayers to be answered, we must not have any unforgiveness toward anyone.

MARK 11:25

25 And when ye stand praying, forgive, if ye have ought against any: that your Father also which is in heaven may forgive you your trespasses.

First Corinthians 13:5 in *The Amplified Bible* says that love "pays no attention to a suffered wrong"!

Notice that Jesus said in Mark 11:25, "... *forgive, if ye have OUGHT against ANY* ...." Not long ago I was sitting in church, listening to a powerful sermon on love. The preacher kept emphasizing that many of us may have some "oughts" and "anys" and perhaps we are noticing suffered wrongs.

Well, her statements hit me right between the eyes. Whenever I spend time with the Lord in prayer, I try to check my heart to make sure I have forgiven anyone who may have wronged me in any way.

To be honest with you, when I checked my heart that day, I could find no unforgiveness in there. That's not to say I haven't ever had to forgive anyone. I've had to do that many times! I was just making sure there were no traces of unforgiveness in my heart.

That day I was cruising along, feeling as though I was doing pretty well in my love walk, until the preacher said, "We shouldn't even be *noticing* suffered wrongs." Well, let me tell you, I had forgiven people, but I definitely had been noticing!

I realized I had the bigger issues covered . . . bigger to me, that is. But I was letting the "little things" slide, not realizing they were even there, thinking they were no big deal. I saw that I had a couple of little "oughts" and "anys" I had to clear up in prayer.

The devil will always try to bring little "oughts" and "anys" across your path. For example, you might be in church and someone you know doesn't say hello to you, so you leave church feeling slighted. Guess what? You just noticed a suffered wrong!

Love Pays No Attention

The Lord has dealt with me many times concerning areas where I have missed it in my love walk. Even though the Bible tells us that love is not supposed to notice a suffered wrong, I recall a time when I *did* take notice and really yielded to the flesh.

I had just finished writing a brand-new book and the publishing company had mailed me a copy of the cover. I was really excited about it. The cover was sitting out on my kitchen table when someone saw it, picked it up, looked at it, and said, "This is the ugliest book cover I have ever seen in my entire life."

You can imagine what went through my mind. The books were already being printed. It was too late to change the cover. To tell you the truth, the cover was fine. I really think their comment just came out of their own insecurities.

I could have kept myself from getting offended. But I paid *great* attention to this suffered wrong, and instead of walking in love, I retaliated with a "dig" of my own. I said, "Well, one Christian bookstore pre-ordered and bought 4,000 copies because they liked the cover so much. That's a pretty good sale for the ugliest-looking cover you've ever seen!"

I just *had* to open my big mouth and try to make myself look good. But when I did, something happened. I was extremely convicted by the Holy Spirit, and I asked the Lord to forgive me right on the spot. I had let my flesh get the best of me by putting a little "dig" in to let them know how many of my books had been sold. But if I had been walking in love, I would have paid no attention to this suffered wrong and just let it go.

Love Doesn't Keep Score

1 CORINTHIANS 13:5 (*NIV*)

5 It [love] is not rude, it is not self-seeking, it is not easily angered, it keeps no record of wrongs.

Notice that love doesn't keep a record when someone has done them wrong. Imagine what it would be like if the Lord kept a record of all of our sins and didn't erase them or forget them. Boy, would we be in a mess! So don't allow bitterness to set in. I like the saying, "You can be bitter, or you can be better, but you can't be both." One person said that harboring unforgiveness toward someone is like you drinking poison and expecting the other person to get sick!

Thank God for the blood of Jesus. First John 1:9 tells us, *"If we confess our sins, he is faithful and just to forgive us our sins, and to cleanse us from all unrighteousness."* And in Hebrews 10:17 God says, *"Their sins and iniquities will I remember no more."*

When you ask God to forgive you, He never remembers your sin ever again! Psalm 103:12 says, *"As far as the east is from the west, so far hath he removed our transgressions from us."*

If you are driving east and you keep driving east, do you ever hit west? No, never! That's what the Lord means. He will never remember your sin again.

If God doesn't keep score or records of our wrongs, then neither should we. Are you keeping a record? Are you keeping score and counting the suffered wrongs? Do you keep reminding your spouse of some way they hurt you years ago and you won't let it go? If you are doing that, it's time to let it go. Once you forgive someone of something, you should never bring it up again.

MARK 11:25 (*Amplified*)

25 And whenever you stand praying, if you have anything against anyone, forgive him and let it drop (leave it, let it go), in order that your Father Who is in heaven may also forgive you your [own] failings and shortcomings and let them drop.

This scripture tells us that we should leave an offense, drop it, and let it go. That means we should stop talking about it! We shouldn't bring it up anymore. We shouldn't keep score anymore. Forgiveness is a gift given to those who don't deserve it. God gives it to us, and we can give it to others. When we forgive, it's like canceling a debt. We tear up the piece of paper in our mind,

> Forgiveness is a gift given to those who don't deserve it.

just like we would a loan agreement. When we cancel the debt, the person owes us nothing! Not one dime. That means, as far as we are concerned, the other person does not even owe us an apology. The debt has been canceled.

Don't Rob Yourself of a Blessing

One time I discovered that I had been keeping score in a different way. I was helping someone out and they didn't appreciate it. I noticed how ungrateful they were and started keeping track of their ungrateful attitude.

I was helping this person out because they didn't have a lot of money. I treated them to expensive dinners several times, among other things. I noticed that each time we went out to eat, they never thanked me for buying their meal. Not once.

As their not saying thanks became more frequent, I thought to myself, *I wonder if they're ever going to say thank you. I'm just going to count and see how many times I buy their meal before they say thank you.*

One day I was telling my mother how much money I had spent on this person and how they had never once thanked me. I expected her to sympathize with me, but instead my mom said, "Kate, you're keeping score! And besides that, you're robbing yourself of a blessing because you're wanting to be recognized for what you've done and therefore your motive in giving is wrong."

Ouch! She was right! Don't misunderstand me. I do believe that when someone blesses us, we *should* be thankful. However, when we're the ones doing the blessing, we shouldn't be looking for things in return from them, but from God. When we give, it should be with no strings attached.

Give People the Benefit of the Doubt

Has anyone ever caused you to notice a suffered wrong that you hadn't noticed before? You didn't even think about it until they brought it up, and then you thought, *Hey! Yeah, they should have treated me better!*

One time the Lord revealed to me how I had allowed this to happen in my own life. A few months after my mother moved to Heaven, I was really missing her. Not only was she a great mother, but she was my best friend.

I had been thinking about all the wonderful love and support that was poured out toward me from ministers, partners, and friends all around the world. Beautiful flowers were sent to the funeral home . . . friends and even well-known preachers just encouraged me so much with their love and support. Some of them I didn't even know very well, but words cannot describe how much their care and concern meant to me.

I was feeling overwhelmed by all the love and kindness I had received, *until* someone called me on the phone. This person asked me point-blank if a certain ministry leader who I was close to had ever called or acknowledged my mother's death in any way. I had to answer, "No." The truth was, I hadn't even thought about it until this person asked me.

As I hung up the phone, I started meditating on what this ministry leader *had not done* for me. I thought, *Hey, they're in the ministry, they're supposed to be my friend, and they don't even care that my mother died!*

As I was sitting in church listening to the same message I referred to earlier on love's "oughts" and "anys," the Lord brought this to my attention. He revealed to me that I had *noticed* a suffered wrong and allowed an "ought" and an "any" to enter my own life. An "ought" represents a grudge or unforgiveness, and an "any" simply represents any person.

What I should have done was not take notice. I should have given this friend of mine the benefit of the doubt. Maybe they were going through a very difficult time in their own life. Besides that, how did I know that they hadn't been praying for me and my family?

Most importantly, it's not my job to see to it that someone else is walking in love toward me. It's my job to see to it that *I* am walking in love toward *them*. Besides that, it's really none of my business what they do or how they act.

All that aside, the person who called me and caused me to notice a suffered wrong should never have done that. They really shouldn't have brought the matter to my attention. They were just being petty, and we really have to watch out how much time we spend with people like that. The devil was using them and they didn't even know it.

Likewise, we should see to it that we don't allow the devil to use us to do this same thing to someone else. It's time that we all grow up. I trust that telling you my own shortcomings might just make you feel a whole lot better when you miss it.

Get Your Mind Off of Yourself and Bless Someone Else

Thinking about what this ministry leader should have done for me really wasn't yielding to the love of God.

Besides that, if we meditate on what people haven't done for us, the truth is, we're being selfish and self-centered and feeling sorry for ourselves. We need to get our mind off of ourselves and bless someone else.

A woman I know recently lost her mother, and right after I lost my mother I spent a lot of time on the phone encouraging her, praying with her, and supporting her in any way I could. As a result of sowing love to her, I found that God started helping me. That's what can happen when you get your mind off of yourself and walk in love.

Faith Works by Love

As a matter of fact, our love walk is *so* important that without it, our faith won't work.

GALATIANS 5:6

6 For in Jesus Christ neither circumcision availeth any thing, nor uncircumcision; but faith which worketh by love.

We can have all these other habits down pat and even perfected. But if we're not walking in love, nothing is going to operate effectively in our life.

One day I was praying the love scriptures from First Corinthians 13:4–8 from *The Amplified Bible*. I substituted my name for the word "love" every time it was used. Where it states, "Love is kind," I said, "Kate is kind." Where it says, "Love is patient," I said, "Kate is patient." You get the picture. (Making these confessions would be a great thing for you to do as well.)

I was feeling so good about myself that morning concerning this area of walking in love toward people. I was loving everyone that day! Of course, it's very easy to walk in love when no one else is home! I got ready to go to the office, still reciting some of those beautiful scriptures: "Love beareth all things, believeth all things, hopeth all things, endureth all things. *Kate* bears all things, believes all things, hopes all things, endures all things." I was really feeling good.

I got into my new car that morning feeling all full of God's love. I decided to pick up my mail at the post office and was reading a letter in the parking lot. As I was sitting in my brand-new car reading through my mail, a lady pulled up alongside me, opened her door, and smashed her door into mine!

I pretty much ignored it, thinking that she accidentally hit my door. So I continued to read my letter. All of a sudden she did it again! I thought, *That lady is just not having a good day.*

The third time, the lady made sure that I was looking and *on purpose* she smashed my car door with her not-so-new car. She hit my door, slammed her door shut, then said some things to me that I won't repeat and stomped off mad into the post office.

Remember, just five minutes before all of this happened, I loved everybody! Now suddenly I didn't feel so loving. In fact, I began meditating on what I was going to say to this woman when she came out of the post office! Apparently I had parked too close to the line, not leaving her enough room to get out of her car comfortably, and it upset her.

So there I was—presented with an opportunity to walk in the love of God that I had been speaking over myself earlier that day. I have found that it is really easy to walk in love when you're by yourself. When everyone else shows up, it's more difficult. It's also easy to walk in love when people are sweet and kind to you. However, the time we really need to exercise our love walk is when someone *isn't* kind to us, like that lady I encountered at the post office.

Hurting People Hurt People

Really, it's our choice whether we are going to walk in love or yield to our flesh. I asked myself, "What would love do in this situation?" We should ask ourselves that when faced with a challenging circumstance.

Well, love sure enough wouldn't get into a fight with this lady about a car door. I could already see the newspaper headlines: "Local Evangelist Beats Up Woman at Post Office." I decided the best thing to do was to avoid a confrontation. Yes, this was my brand-new car, but cars are not more important than people. I spent time after that really praying for her.

Obviously that woman was hurting. If my parking too close to the line upset her that much, she must really have needed my prayers. Have you ever heard the saying, "Hurting people hurt people"? We don't know what people are going through. Perhaps she'd just lost a loved one. She might have been on her way to the hospital to visit her husband who was terminally ill. Or maybe she was going through a divorce. We don't always know what motivates people to do unpleasant things, but you can be sure there usually is a reason.

That's why it's so important for us as Christians to have compassion for others and show them the love of God. Forbearance is a godly characteristic. The more you grow in the love of God, the stronger you will become spiritually, and the more victory you will see in your life. Make it your habit to develop a strong love walk because the Bible says, "Love never fails!" (1 Cor. 13:8).

Of the seven habits we have talked about in this book, this is by far the most important. The Bible says that people will know we are Christians by the love we have for each other (John 13:34–35). Let's show people the love of God by reaching out with His love. Love really is the key to gaining victory and becoming an uncommon achiever.

Take Action Now

Things I will do this week to grow in my love walk:

_____

_____

_____

_____

_____

_____

_____

_____

_____

_____

_____

_____

_____

_____

_____

_____

_____

_____

_____

_____

Develop the 7 Habits

But be ye doers of the word, and not hearers only,
deceiving your own selves.

—James 1:22

Congratulations! You have just completed this book. That alone is a big step toward cultivating another great habit—reading.

In this book we have looked at seven habits of uncommon achievers. These are seven prime habits that will make a significant difference in your life as you develop and practice them. The Lord will give you your own habits as well. This is just a starting place for you.

As you put these seven habits into practice, you'll begin to see great changes. Remember: change doesn't come overnight, but it does come! Your life can change as you act on God's Word.

At the beginning of this book, I mentioned that it takes 21 consecutive days to form a habit. On page 111 you'll find a chart that you can use to record your progress in forming the habits I've talked about. You can focus on one habit at a time, or you can work on more than one. Check the boxes for the days you worked on each habit.

After a while, the things you practice daily will become second nature to you; they will become new habits. Now go to work, and you will stand amazed at what God will do for you!

Remember that the Greater One lives in you! The Holy Spirit in you will help you to develop godly habits that will make a big difference in your life. God has called you to greatness. He has called you to be an uncommon achiever!

21-Day Progress Chart

	Habit #1	Habit #2	Habit #3	Habit #4	Habit #5	Habit #6	Habit #7
	Write Goals	Pray	Strong Spirit	Organize	Control Thoughts	Positive Words	Walk in Love
1							
2							
3							
4							
5							
6							
7							
8							
9							
10							
11							
12							
13							
14							
15							
16							
17							
18							
19							
20							
21							

My Prayer for You

Let me pray for you right now . . .

Heavenly Father, I pray for my friend who is reading this book. They want to change and see You move in their life. Lord, I ask that You help them develop these seven habits and overcome any destructive habits in their life. I take authority over any bad habits that have them bound and I call them *free* in Jesus' Name! Lord, thank You for helping my friend to realize that they are more than a conqueror through Jesus Christ Who loves them! I pray that You will cause my friend to become highly motivated to put these seven habits to work in their life today. May they never again be the same, in Jesus' Name. Amen.

About the Author

Rev. Kate McVeigh ministers extensively throughout the United States and abroad, preaching the Gospel of Jesus Christ with signs and wonders following. Her outreach ministry includes books, teaching tapes, and a daily radio broadcast, *The Voice of Faith*, as well as her weekly television broadcast, which airs throughout the United States.

Kate is known as an evangelist and teacher of the Gospel well-grounded in the Word of God, with a powerful anointing to heal the sick and win the lost. Through Kate's down-to-earth and often humorous teaching of the Word, many are motivated to attain God's best for their lives.

To contact Kate McVeigh or receive a free product catalog of other books and ministry materials, use the following information:

Kate McVeigh Ministries

P.O. Box 1688

Warren, MI 48090-1688

(586) 795-8885

www.katemcveigh.org

Important Message

If you have never met Jesus Christ and received Him as your Savior, you can know Him today. God cares for you and wants to help you in every area of your life. That is why He sent Jesus to die for you. You can make your life right with God this very moment and make Heaven your home.

Pray this prayer now:

God, I ask You to forgive me of my sins. I believe You sent Jesus to die on the cross for me. I receive Jesus Christ as my personal Lord and Savior. I confess Him as Lord of my life and I give my life to Him. Thank You, Lord, for saving me and for making me new. In Jesus' Name, amen.

If you prayed this prayer, welcome to the family of God!

Please let me know about your decision for Jesus. I want to send you some free literature to help you in your new walk with the Lord.